Maryland Bucket List Adventure Guide

Explore 100 Offbeat Destinations You Must Visit!

Kathy Reed

Canyon Press
canyon@purplelink.org

Please consider writing a review!
Just visit: purplelink.org/review

ISBN: 978-1-957590-04-2

FREE BONUS

Discover 31 Incredible Places You Can
Visit Next! Just Go To:

purplelink.org/travel

Table of Contents

Centerville

Chesapeake Beach

College Park

Columbia

Cumberland

Dorchester County

Ellicott City

Essex

How to Use This Book

Welcome to your very own adventure guide to exploring the many wonders of the state of Maryland. Not only does this book lay out the most wonderful places to visit and sights to see in the vast state, but it provides addresses and GPS coordinates for Google Maps to make exploring that much easier.

Adventure Guide
Sorted by region, this guide offers over 100 amazing wonders found in Maryland for you to go see and explore. These can be visited in any order, and this book will help keep track of where you've been and where to look forward to going next. Each portion describes the area or place, what to look for, its location address, and what you may need to bring along.

GPS Coordinates
As you can imagine, not all of the locations in this book have a physical address. Fortunately, some of our listed wonders are either located within a National Park or Reserve, or are near a city, town, or place of business. For those that are not associated with a specific location, it is easiest to map it using GPS coordinates.

Luckily, Google has a system of codes that converts the coordinates into pin drop locations that Google Maps is able to interpret and navigate.

Each adventure in this guide will include both the GPS coordinates along with site addresses to help you find the location.

It is important that you are prepared for poor cell signals. It is recommended to route your location and ensure that the directions are accessible offline. Depending on your device and the distance of some locations, you may need to travel with a backup battery source.

About Maryland

The recorded colonial history of Maryland starts in 1498, when the first Europeans caught sight of the Maryland coast. In reality, Maryland was the home of Native Americans long before colonization, and the harbor played an integral role in their survival.

Fishing and aquaculture, namely oysters, were a main source of food, along with hunting and farming. The Susquehannock and Piscataway Tribes dominated most of the area around the harbor, the Chesapeake Bay, and the Potomac River. It was the chief of the Piscataway who permitted the early colonists to settle in the area in the 17th century.

Maryland officially became a colony when George Calvert, also known as 1st Baron Baltimore or Lord Baltimore, sought a charter from the British king. While Lord Baltimore originally wanted to name the territory Crescentia, meaning Land of Growth, King Charles I decreed it be called Terra Mariae, or Maryland.

Today, Baltimore is the most populous city in Maryland and one of the country's 30 most populated cities. It is home to the famous Baltimore & Ohio (B&O) Railroad, the first and oldest common rail line in the United States.

The Inner Harbor continues to shape the state just as it has throughout history. From providing sustenance to Native Americans and early colonists, to acting as a major military seaport during the Revolutionary and Civil Wars, Baltimore's Inner Harbor today is a zeitgeist of history, culture, and education. The National Aquarium, the *USS*

Constellation, and the Maryland Science Center are just a taste of what the harbor has to offer. Explore more history and art throughout the Old Line State by visiting all the stops in this book.

Landscape and Climate

You are in for two very different weather experiences depending on where you visit in Maryland. In the western part of the state — areas like Cumberland, Hagerstown, and Frederick — you are more likely to experience mild, continental weather, with highs only reaching 65°F in July.

However, cities like Baltimore and Annapolis will experience a humid, almost subtropical climate on the eastern seaboard thanks to the Atlantic Ocean and the Chesapeake Bay. Highs here can reach well over 100°F in the summer.

If hiking, camping, and outdoor adventures are on your vacation bucket list, consider visiting the Maryland coast during late spring or early fall to avoid the muggy weather.

Maryland's coastal tendencies also influence its landscape, and visitors are welcome to explore the wetlands, the islands, the Coastal Plains, and the Appalachian Mountains. The highest point in Maryland is Backbone Mountain at 3,360 feet, while the lowest point at the Chesapeake Bay is barely 100 feet above sea level.

The Coastal Plains and Maryland's coast have a very interesting relationship. In the northern part of the state, the Plains are fertile and provide ample growth opportunities for verdant evergreens, oaks, laurels, and magnolias. But in

4

the south, the Plains' sandy, salty marshlands continue to fall victim to erosion, both natural and man-made.

Considering that St. Clement's Island is only 1/10th of its original size due to the ever-changing Chesapeake shoreline, the state government and the Maryland Department of Natural Resources have created breakwaters to protect the shore from wave erosion. They prepare annual resources for residents and visitors to learn more about coastal erosion and how to prepare and protect their property.

Blackwater National Wildlife Refuge

Blackwater National Wildlife Refuge (BNWR) is home to a unique combination of animals that make their homes in the forest, marsh, or shallow water areas in the state. The BNWR was initially established as a refuge for migratory birds but has since evolved to protect fox squirrels, bald eagles, and more. The diversity of wildlife living here, and the fact that much of the refuge is made up of wetlands, is why many people call BNWR the "Everglades of the North."

Visitors can hike, bike, or drive the 6.5-mile paved Wildlife Drive loop or stop in the visitor center for a look through the eagle and osprey cams. There are additional hiking trails, including three paddling trails for kayaks and canoes, throughout the refuge. Seasonal hunting, fishing, and crabbing are also allowed with the appropriate licenses.

Best time to visit: Fall and winter between October and January

Pass/Permit/Fees: $3 per vehicle; $1 per person; free for 16 and under

Closest city or town: Algonquin

Address: Visitor Center is located at 2145 Key Wallace Dr., Cambridge, MD 21613

GPS Coordinates: 38.4220° N, 76.0624° W

Did You Know? BNWR helped rehabilitate the Delmarva Peninsula fox squirrel population, and they were removed from the endangered list in 2015.

Bacon Ridge Trail

Bacon Ridge Trail is tucked neatly inside the 900-acre Bacon Ridge Natural Area, a county-protected conservation area. The park is open to the public and offers a few attractions beyond the hiking trail, including a historical cemetery and the remains of an old watermill.

The Bacon Ridge Trail itself is a 6-mile loop through the forest with a few hills. The trail is fairly moderate but poorly marked in places, so you may have to adjust and find your way back onto the route a few times. As conservation efforts continue in Bacon Ridge, the county has documented 16 distinct archaeological sites in the park, including Native American campsites and 18th-century structures, though they are not open to the public.

Best time to visit: Late spring or early fall

Pass/Permit/Fees: Free to hike and bike

Closest city or town: Annapolis

Address: 1801 Hawkins Rd., Annapolis, MD 21401

GPS Coordinates: 39.0363° N, 76.6211° W

Did You Know? The trail was originally built in 2015 as a 2.5-mile hike off Hawkins Road. The additional 4 miles were added in 2016.

Chesapeake Bay

The Chesapeake Bay is the largest and likely oldest estuary in the United States. Fishing and boating were the main sources of Maryland's early economy, and visitors today can partake in the same maritime adventures. Try your hand at fishing, crabbing, or oyster farming, or at least get a taste of the delicious blue crab. Enjoy other natural wonders by spying on wildlife in the tidal wetlands, soaking up the sun on the beach, or fishing on the miles of open water.

There are many different spots to see at the Chesapeake Bay in Maryland, each offering a unique perspective. Visit Annapolis or Baltimore for a more urban and historical view of the Bay or stay in Cape Charles or Chesapeake Beach for a quieter coastal experience. Visitors are always welcome to sail and kayak from the appropriate docks.

Best time to visit: Weekdays

Pass/Permit/Fees: $16 per person, $10 for military, $9 for locals

Closest city or town: Annapolis

Address: 3330 Chesapeake Beach Rd., Chesapeake Beach, MD 20732

GPS Coordinates: 38.6948° N, 76.5337° W

Did You Know? The Bay was created 650 million years ago when a meteor crashed into the Atlantic, creating 441 separate craters.

Kent Island

With all the beaches in Maryland, it can be hard to choose just one to visit. If you're traveling with a dog, Kent Island is an excellent choice. The two beaches at Kent Island offer amazing views of the Chesapeake Bay Bridge, but only one is exclusively dog friendly. To find the dog beach, head to the Matapeake Fishing Pier and follow signs for the Dogwood Pet Retreat. You can access the other beach at Terrapin Nature Park by following the white path of crushed oyster shells. Stick to the wider path to find the water or follow the narrow path for a short 2.8-mile hike into the wetlands and wildlife habitat.

Originally, the island was used to farm tobacco and corn. However, thanks to the construction of the Bay Bridge, it became a resort town by the end of the 19th century. But you can still see remnants of the colonial crops in the tidal basin at Terrapin.

Best time to visit: Summer

Pass/Permit/Fees: Free

Closest city or town: Annapolis

Address: Visitor Center is located at 425 Piney Narrows Rd., Chester, MD 21619

GPS Coordinates: 38.9373° N, 76.3290° W

Did You Know? Virginia and Maryland both fought over which colony Kent Island belonged to.

Matapeake Beach

Matapeake Beach on Kent Island features a historic clubhouse and access to a quiet spot on the shore of the Chesapeake Bay. The clubhouse is mainly reserved for weddings and other special events, but visitors can cool off with a sweet treat and rent beach chairs and umbrellas from the facility. The clubhouse was originally a ferry terminal for travelers working their way up and down the Bay, but the original building collapsed during a blizzard in 2003 and was rebuilt into the structure you can visit today.

Dogs and pets are not allowed at the clubhouse or public beach nearby, but Matapeake Beach features areas that are dog-friendly. A short hiking trail starts at the clubhouse fence and winds through the woods, ending at the shores of the dog beach. Release the reins and let your hound kick up the sand and chase a few waves while you relax in the sun.

Best time to visit: Summer, but off-season rentals are available

Pass/Permit/Fees: Beach is free; $10 to use the pier and boat ramp

Closest city or town: Annapolis

Address: 2010 Sonny Schulz Blvd., Stevensville, MD 21666

GPS Coordinates: 38.9564° N, 76.3532° W

Did You Know? The fishing pier used to be the landing for the Chesapeake Bay Ferry System.

Old Town Annapolis and William Paca House

William Paca was one of four Marylanders to sign the Declaration of Independence, and his estate — constructed in the 1760s — is one of the most well-preserved 18th-century homes in the country. The former governor's mansion features period furnishings, motifs, and moldings. The William Paca House is just a five-minute walk from historic downtown Annapolis. Both Old Town Annapolis and the William Paca House are historical and cultural epicenters today. The house passed through many hands and families over the centuries, and was even converted to a hotel called Carvel Hall at one point.

Best time to visit: Mornings; William Paca House Museum opens at 10 a.m.

Pass/Permit/Fees: $10 per adult, $9 for seniors, $5 for children

Closest city or town: Annapolis

Address: 186 Prince George St., Annapolis, MD 21401

GPS Coordinates: 38.9796° N, 76.4879° W

Did You Know? The part of the home that was Carvel Hall Hotel was demolished to return the house to its original appearance.

Sandy Point State Park

You'll forget you're only seconds from D.C. when visiting the tranquil Sandy Point State Park. It is a popular beach destination in the summer, with its amazing views of the Chesapeake Bay Bridge (you can practically swim underneath it) and 22 boat ramps that get you out on the water as quickly as possible. Animal lovers and birdwatchers should hike the Symbi and Blue Crab Trails to catch sight of local wildlife, including owls, opossums, hawks, rabbits, and more. Fishing is also permitted anywhere in the park, from the ponds to the Chesapeake Bay, but crabbing is restricted to certain days of the week.

While Sandy Point is a popular spot in the summer, it also hosts numerous events during the fall and winter months that shouldn't be missed. The annual Maryland Seafood Festival takes place every September, with live music, local vendors, and delicious food; and Lights on the Bay illuminates the Chesapeake Bay during the holidays.

Best time to visit: September - December

Pass/Permit/Fees: $4 per person on weekdays, $5 on weekends and holidays

Closest city or town: Annapolis

Address: 1100 E. College Pkwy., Annapolis, MD 21409

GPS Coordinates: 39.0202° N, 76.4090° W

Did You Know? Sandy Point was the first public beach to be desegregated in 1955.

U.S. Naval Academy Museum and Chapel

The U.S. Naval Academy is one the oldest and most prestigious academies that military officers can attend. The museum is one of the oldest in the nation as well, started in 1845 when President Polk ordered old Navy flags sent to the Academy. The Navy continues to send all manner of artifacts to the academy's museum, from paintings and portraits to model ships and medals. Visitors can follow the history of naval combat from the 16th century into WWII through the Beverly R. Robinson Collection and learn more about ship instruments, gear, uniforms, and weapons used by early soldiers.

Nearby, the U.S. Naval Academy Chapel is an icon along the Annapolis skyline. The dome, designed by Ernest Flagg, is covered in copper and crowns the 193-foot cupola above the altar. Beneath the chapel is the crypt of America's first Naval Commander, John Paul Jones.

Best time to visit: Spring

Pass/Permit/Fees: Free

Closest city or town: Annapolis

Address: 118 Maryland Ave., Annapolis, MD 21402

GPS Coordinates: 38.9828° N, 76.4872° W

Did You Know? The Naval Academy class of 1942 actually graduated in 1941 to support the war effort.

American Visionary Art Museum

Visionary arts feature works created by self-taught artists, inspired by their personal experiences. Every exhibit at the American Visionary Art Museum emphasizes the intuition involved in the creative process rather than formal training.

Permanent exhibits feature the surreal sculptures of Ho Baron, found object artworks by Leo Sewell, and creations from Gregory Warmack. Seasonal events include outdoor sculpture tours, galas, scavenger hunts, and workshops. Events and exhibits change throughout the year, so plan your visit ahead of time if there is an artist you want to see or an event you want to attend. Museum tickets are available online.

Best time to visit: Saturday and Sunday mornings

Pass/Permit/Fees: $16 per adult; $14 for seniors; $10 for student/child

Closest city or town: Baltimore

Address: 800 Key Hwy., Baltimore, MD 21230

GPS Coordinates: 39.2800° N, 76.6069° W

Did You Know? In order to build the museum, community organizers were required to clean copper waste left behind from the former refinery.

Baltimore & Ohio Railroad Museum

The B&O Railroad is the oldest in the country and was the first-ever common rail service carrying passengers and freight across the country. The B&O Railroad Museum is an homage to the railroading era of American history. What began as a 19th century trade show evolved into a historical exhibit of transportation and technology, preserving the railroad for generations to come.

Visitors today can still catch a ride on the B&O every weekend at 11:30 a.m. (1 p.m. on Sundays). The 20-minute ride takes you across the first commercial mile of track laid in the United States. If you happen to visit during the winter, you're in for a special treat of hot chocolate!

Best time to visit: April - January to ride the train

Pass/Permit/Fees: $20 for adults, $17 for seniors, $12 for children

Closest city or town: Baltimore

Address: 901 W. Pratt St., Baltimore, MD 21223

GPS Coordinates: 39.2855° N, 76.6326° W

Did You Know? A conductor of the B&O Railroad alerted the U.S. Military of John Brown's raid on Harpers Ferry in 1859.

Baltimore Basilica

The Baltimore Basilica, also known as the Basilica of the National Shrine of the Assumption of the Blessed Virgin Mary, is one of the most beautiful buildings in Baltimore. Its beauty is a big part of why this Roman Catholic monument is one of the most popular spots in the city. No matter your faith, a free self-guided tour through the 19th-century cathedral is a must.

Take your time and enjoy the view of the iconic Ionic columns at the entrance from a seat out front. Then enter the church and look upward to take in the dome (suggested by Thomas Jefferson) and the artwork painted into the ceiling. Walk the church to see more 18th- and 19th-century paintings, gifted by King Louis XVIII; then take a seat in a pew. The view to the altar perfectly encapsulates the geometric vision of Benjamin Henry Latrobe, the first professionally trained architect in America. As a good friend of Thomas Jefferson, Latrobe also designed the U.S. Capitol.

Best time to visit: Weekday mornings between Mass times

Pass/Permit/Fees: Free

Closest city or town: Baltimore

Address: 409 Cathedral St., Baltimore, MD 21201

GPS Coordinates: 39.2944° N, 76.6162° W

Did You Know? The Baltimore Basilica is the largest Roman Catholic Church in North America.

Baltimore Inner Harbor

Baltimore Inner Harbor offers many exciting activities along with an ocean view and harbor strolls. Historical boat tours of the USS *Constellation*, the oldest sail-only warship left in the country, and the USS *Torsk*, a ten-torpedo trench-class submarine from WWII, are available at the harbor. Tours provide an in-depth look at both the military tactics of the era and modern restoration techniques.

Other ways to explore the water include Spirit Cruises, which offer history tours, spirits, and rooftop games all in one place, and Baltimore Cruises, which provide different types of water tours for different groups.

Best time to visit: June - August

Pass/Permit/Fees: To ride the historic ships: $15 for adults, $13 for seniors and students, $7 for children; under 5 are free

Closest city or town: Baltimore

Address: 561 Light St., Baltimore, MD 21202

GPS Coordinates: 39.2858° N, 76.6131° W

Did You Know? During the 1970s and '80s, Inner Harbor was a model for urban development in other major cities.

Baltimore Museum of Art

If Henri Matisse has a home outside of France, it is at the Baltimore Museum of Art. One thousand of his paintings adorn the walls that also showcase ancient Antioch pieces, textiles from across the globe, and paintings by Matisse's contemporaries, including Picasso and Renoir.

At the heart of the museum is the Cone Collection, a selection of paintings and art once owned by the Cone sisters, Etta and Claribel. The socialite sisters were close friends of Matisse and Picasso and donated the collection of their works and more to the museum after their deaths. Having been built over a century ago, a visit to the Baltimore Museum of Art means walking in the footsteps of these famous art collectors who would often lend their works to the museum while they were still alive.

Best time to visit: Museum opens at 10, and passes are available every 30 minutes. Come early to avoid crowds and longer wait times.

Pass/Permit/Fees: Free

Closest city or town: Baltimore

Address: 10 Art Museum Dr., Baltimore, MD

GPS Coordinates: 39.3262° N, 76.6193° W

Did You Know? The museum is modeled after the Metropolitan Museum of Art in New York and the Museum of Fine Arts in Boston.

Earth Treks

No matter the weather, rock climbers can hit the walls at Earth Treks. Earth Treks rock climbing gyms are located across the state in Columbia, Rockville, Lutherville-Timonium, and Baltimore, giving visitors plenty of opportunities for this activity.

Routes change twice a month to keep things fresh, and climbers can train for outdoor climbing, get their heart rate up, or just hang out with friends on the wall. Beginners can learn how to climb with instructors at the gym, and non-climbers can sign up for a yoga class or workout session.

If you're already a member, you can visit any of the Earth Trek locations throughout Maryland and qualify for free guest passes for your friends and family. Check the gym's events calendar before you visit to see what kinds of classes and events are available.

Best time to visit: Mid-afternoon

Pass/Permit/Fees: $22 per day pass

Closest city or town: Baltimore

Address: 1700 W. 41st St. #440, Baltimore, MD 21211

GPS Coordinates: 39.3360° N, 76.6437° W

Did You Know? It takes the crew four hours to build 4-5 climbing routes and another two hours to test run them.

Edgar Allan Poe House & Museum

The brick home at 203 North Amity Street is the original home where Edgar Allan Poe lived with his aunt, grandmother, and cousins during the 1830s. The home is unfurnished and has been left untouched since 1835. While the rooms of the home are empty, the exhibits within do include Poe's writing desk, chair, telescope, and the glassware used by the family while they were living there. Exhibits do change and travel throughout the year, so check the museum's calendar for special events like the annual Edgar Allan Poe Festival in October.

The home itself is an icon of the architecture at the time and is one of the few 19th-century brick row houses left after the block was scheduled for demolition in the 1930s. The home still retains most of its original woodwork, and visitors are invited to climb the narrow staircase into the attic that was likely Poe's room while he lived here.

Best time to visit: September and October

Pass/Permit/Fees: $10 per adult, $8 for seniors, $5 for children

Closest city or town: Baltimore

Address: 203 N. Amity St., Baltimore, MD 21223

GPS Coordinates: 39.2913° N, 76.6353° W

Did You Know? Poe's love of cryptograms and sending them to local papers popularized puzzles in newspapers, something we still see today.

Fell's Point

Fell's Point is the oldest neighborhood in Baltimore, and one of the oldest in the country. It's earmarked as a National Historic District and boasts some of the oldest American historical buildings, including the Robert Long House and the Broadway Market. Today, Fell's Point is a one-stop destination for hotels, fine and local dining, museums, historical tours, and annual festivals.

Learn about its history at the Frederick Douglass-Isaac Myers Maritime Park Museum before enjoying a pint at The Horse You Came In On Saloon. In fact, there are over 120 pubs in Fell's Point, and the neighborhood is known for having more bars and restaurants per square foot than anywhere else in Maryland. If you come for the holidays, don't miss the annual Halloween and Old Tyme Christmas festivals.

Best time to visit: Fall

Pass/Permit/Fees: Free

Closest city or town: Baltimore

Address: 1710 Thames St., Baltimore, MD

GPS Coordinates: 39.2842° N, 76.5938° W

Did You Know? The Horse You Came In On Saloon is the oldest bar in Baltimore and was Edgar Allan Poe's last stop before he died.

Fort McHenry National Monument

A port as popular and busy as Baltimore needed a proper fort to protect it, In 1798, Fort McHenry replaced the former Revolutionary War-era Fort Whetstone to better defend the harbor. The upgrade proved useful when the British attempted to invade here in September 1814, inspiring Francis Scott Key to pen the Star-Spangled Banner. The Visitor and Education Center at the fort tells the story of the War of 1812 and the fort's later roles in WWI.

Exhibits include 19th-century artifacts found on-site, including the same flag Key wrote about, and a ten-minute mini-movie about the Battle of Baltimore. The Education Room focuses primarily on the medical advancements made by the military hospital here during WWI. Nearby, visitors can hike a bit of the 560-mile Star-Spangled Banner National Historic Trail for more historical sites, museums, and forts.

Best time to visit: Spring or fall

Pass/Permit/Fees: $15 per adult; free for children 15 and under

Closest city or town: Baltimore

Address: 2400 E. Fort Ave., Baltimore, MD 21230

GPS Coordinates: 39.2633° N, 76.5799° W

Did You Know? Fort McHenry was named after James McHenry, who served as Secretary of War for Presidents Washington and Adams.

Gwynns Falls Trail

You wouldn't know it, walking in downtown Baltimore, but a hiking trail actually runs through the heart of this city. Gwynns Falls Trail starts at Gwynns Falls Leakin Park and snakes through downtown, sometimes using side streets and on-street pathways. Hikers and bikers can choose to cruise the main line of the trail, which is a 10¾-mile path that parallels Light St., or veer off on any of the main line's branches. The most popular are Middle Branch Trail (5 mi), Hutton Trail (1 mi), and Dickeyville Trail (¾ mi).

If you're bringing your bike along, Middle Branch Trail is your best route. It leads you through downtown along the water, connecting you with urban nature routes across the city. But if you prefer a more reflective hike, step onto the Windsor Hill Conservation Trail. It's a quieter, less crowded trail perfect for birdwatching and nature study.

Best time to visit: April and May

Pass/Permit/Fees: Free

Closest city or town: Baltimore

Address: Interstate 70 (I-70) at Security Blvd. Park and Ride, Baltimore, MD

GPS Coordinates: 39.3273° N, 76.7171° W

Did You Know? The free Gwynns Falls Trail app can help you decide which branch of the trail to hike.

Maryland Science Center

The Maryland Science Center offers three floors of discovery. Permanent exhibits feature dinosaurs, laboratory experiments, and a working generator that needs you to power it up. It's also the only place in Baltimore where you'll find an observatory, IMAX theater, and planetarium all in one place. Most everything is hands-on at the science center, and visitors are encouraged to test Newton's theories, follow the lives of blue crabs in the harbor, and ask questions.

Exhibit staff are extremely knowledgeable and can answer queries regarding climate change, disease therapy, and more. Visiting and permanent exhibits feature various live and interactive presentations throughout the day. Topics can vary depending on when you visit, and the center's location at the Inner Harbor also inspires different seasonal events. Presentations and times are posted daily and cover everything from liquid nitrogen to nanotechnology.

Best time to visit: Early morning before it gets too crowded; museum opens at 10 a.m.

Pass/Permit/Fees: $30 per adult, $25 for seniors, $20 for children

Closest city or town: Baltimore

Address: 601 Light St., Baltimore, MD 21230

GPS Coordinates: 39.2755° N, 76.6072° W

Did You Know? Maryland Science Center offers scholarships and awards to young Maryland scientists.

Maryland Zoo in Baltimore

There are five areas to explore at Maryland Zoo, starting with the prairie dog farm at Schaefer Plaza. A playground is nearby where children can run off some steam before heading to the African Journey. Walk through the aviary to see hornbills, spoonbills, pygmy geese, and more before making your way to the watering hole where you're sure to spy flamingos, cranes, storks, and a tortoise or two.

Cross the boardwalk to visit the lions, chimps, lemurs, giraffes, and elephants. The unique Maryland Wilderness Children's Zoo features local creatures, both endangered and invulnerable, as well as a petting zoo. Visitors can also chill out with the polar bears and penguins before hopping a ride on the free tram over to Zoo Central. You can grab a bite to eat, ride the carousel, or hop on the children's train from there.

Best time to visit: Mornings; zoo opens at 10 a.m.

Pass/Permit/Fees: $22 per adult, $19 for seniors, $18 for children

Closest city or town: Baltimore

Address: 1 Safari Pl., Baltimore, MD 21217

GPS Coordinates: 38.3227° N, 76.6498° W

Did You Know? Maryland Zoo is the eighth oldest zoo in the country, although many incorrectly believe it to be the third oldest.

National Aquarium

If you're visiting the Inner Harbor, a stop at the National Aquarium is in order. Stingray petting pools, reptile meet-and-greets, and a trip to the Amazon River Forest are all waiting. Learn more about the jellyfish in Chesapeake Bay or explore the Pacific Coral Reef before venturing to the Amazon and Australian exhibits. It's not just all fish at the aquarium, either. Don't forget to visit your scaly friends at the snake and reptilian exhibits throughout the different sections. Bright-green emerald tree boas are lounging in the Amazon, while death adders and monitors prowl in Australia. The aquarium hosts special events throughout the month, from discount days to 4-D movie experiences, and tickets can be purchased in advance or at the aquarium. Visitors can also sign up for various creature meet-and-greets, including dolphin training classes and diving programs.

Best time to visit: Friday night for half-price on all entrance fees

Pass/Permit/Fees: $40 per adult, $35 for seniors, $25 for children

Closest city or town: Baltimore

Address: 501 E. Pratt St., Baltimore, MD 21202

GPS Coordinates: 39.2854° N, 76.6084° W

Did You Know? The aquarium is the largest tourist attraction in Maryland, holding more than 2.2 million gallons of water.

Oriole Park at Camden Yards

If you're in Baltimore during baseball season, check out an Orioles game at Camden Yards. It's the first baseball stadium to embrace the retro look, which earned it the title of The Ballpark That Forever Changed Baseball. It features brick arches and green-painted exposed steel throughout instead of concrete, as well as iconic green stadium seats. Although the stadium is barely over 30 years old, it has vintage design and historical significance.

Baltimore is the birthplace of Babe Ruth, and his father's café originally stood where center field of Camden Yards now is, bringing the story of Maryland baseball full circle. Camden Yards also features the Babe Ruth Museum's Sports Legends exhibit and an indoor concourse that is open to the field, so you'll never miss a second of the game.

Best time to visit: March - October

Pass/Permit/Fees: $12-$100+ for game tickets

Closest city or town: Baltimore

Address: 333 W. Camden St., Baltimore, MD 21201

GPS Coordinates: 39.2839° N, 76.6216° W

Did You Know? The city quickly decided to build Camden Park after losing the Colts to Indianapolis due to the poor state of the previous Memorial Stadium.

Star-Spangled Banner National Historic Trail

The Star-Spangled Banner National Historic Trail covers nearly 300 miles between Maryland, Virginia, and Washington, D.C. It follows the historic route the British took when they invaded the Chesapeake Bay area during the War of 1812. Stops along the way include famous forts and battle sites, towns raided and burned by the British, and museums. Local spots on the historic trail are in Baltimore, Annapolis, and parts of Southern Maryland along the coast of the Chesapeake Bay.

During the tense three years of the war, the Bay bore the brunt of the British forces, defending a fledgling nation from a global superpower. Start the trail at Fort McHenry in Baltimore, then travel up or down the coast via the Chesapeake Country National Scenic Byway to visit battle sites or hop on the Pride of Baltimore II tall ship for a guided sailing tour.

Best time to visit: Late spring or early summer before the crowds

Pass/Permit/Fees: Free; costs for tours will vary

Closest city or town: Baltimore

Address: 2400 E. Fort Ave., Baltimore, MD 21230

GPS Coordinates: 39.2653° N, 76.5818° W

Did You Know? Early American forces in the war refused to fight outside of their home state.

The Walters Art Museum

The Walters Art Museum began as a father-and-son endeavor when William Thomas and Henry Walters decided to build a museum behind their mansion to showcase their collected artifacts. Upon his death, Henry donated the entire collection, the museum, and the mansion to Baltimore. Today, visitors can see the Walters' collection for free.

Ancient artifacts from Egypt, Nubia, Rome, Panama, Mexico, Japan, and China are showcased, including the oldest wooden image of Buddha. The most famous exhibit in the museum is Henry Walters' medieval art collection which includes stained glass, metal work and textiles, and manuscripts. Pieces from the medieval collection often travel to and with other museums, so if it's missing when you visit, it will likely be there when you come back again.

Best time to visit: September - November

Pass/Permit/Fees: Free

Closest city or town: Baltimore

Address: 600 N. Charles St., Baltimore, MD 21201

GPS Coordinates: 39.2964° N, 76.6165° W

Did You Know? The Walters released 20,000 images of the collected works on a Creative Commons License in 2012, the largest collection from any museum.

Arlington National Cemetery

The Arlington National Cemetery is the final resting place for veterans, military heroes, astronauts, terrorist victims, American leaders, and presidents. John F. Kennedy, Jacqueline Kennedy Onassis, and Thurgood Marshall are just a few of the most famous headstones. Visit the Tomb of the Unknown Soldier and see the changing of the guard, which happens every thirty minutes during the summer and every sixty minutes in the winter. You can tour the memorials for the Space Shuttle *Challenger* and the USS *Maine*, featuring the ship's salvaged mast.

Arlington National Cemetery is one of the most popular spots to visit in the DC-Metro area. It's best to arrive early so as to avoid traffic and crowds.

Best time to visit: Saturday and Sunday mornings

Pass/Permit/Fees: $18 for adults (military $7), $14 for seniors, $10 for children (military $5)

Closest city or town: Bethesda

Address: Arlington National Cemetery, Arlington, VA 22211

GPS Coordinates: 38.8769° N, 77.0708° W

Did You Know? William Henry Christman, a Union soldier who died of measles in 1864, was the first soldier buried at Arlington.

Georgetown Historic District

Give yourself enough time to stroll the old neighborhoods and soak up the ambiance of cobblestone streets and grand estates in Georgetown. There's no need to rush by the colonial buildings or speed along the C&O Canal. To truly appreciate the history here, you have to take your time.

A few key spots to see are the Old Stone House on M Street, which is the oldest home in D.C., the gothic Oak Hill Cemetery Chapel on 30th Street, and the Pope residence on O Street. The Pope residence is the first stop on the district's African American Heritage Trail that spans 15 blocks. The neighborhood provides some modern history as well. Prospect Street features the home from *The Exorcist* where you can walk up the infamous concrete stairs, or pop into The Shops at Georgetown Park where Arnold Schwarzenegger jumped out a window in *True Lies*.

Best time to visit: Fall

Pass/Permit/Fees: $2/hour for street parking

Closest city or town: Bethesda

Address: The Old Stone House is located at 3051 M Street, NW, Georgetown, Washington, D.C.

GPS Coordinates: 38.9097° N, 77.0654° W

Did You Know? Georgetown was abolished as a legal city by Congress in 1895.

The White House

The White House is the home of the American president and one of the most iconic sites in Washington, D.C. Visitors are free to take photos and tour the area outside of the wrought iron gates, but in order to get inside, you must request tickets from your congressman. Ticket requests for the free and self-guided tours can be submitted up to three months in advance but no less than 21 days early. Tickets are available on a first-come-first-serve basis, and there are no same-day tickets available.

If you plan on touring the White House, choose your dates ahead of time and book as early as possible. The entire White House is not open to the public, but visitors are allowed to explore the East Wing, including the State Dining Room and the White House Rose Garden. Secret Service agents are posted in each room on the tour to answer questions about architecture, design, and history.

Best time to visit: March - May

Pass/Permit/Fees: Tours are free but must be scheduled in advance.

Closest city or town: Bethesda

Address: 1600 Pennsylvania Ave., NW, Washington, D.C. 20500

GPS Coordinates: 38.8977° N, 77.0365° W

Did You Know? Every president has lived and worked in the White House except George Washington.

Washington, D.C. Temple

The Mormon Temple in Washington, D.C., is the first Mormon church built on the East Coast. Its design is based on the Temple in Salt Lake City, built with six spires representing the Aaronic and Melchizedek priesthoods of the faith.

Along with its stark-white architecture, the landscaping is something to behold. A brand-new fountain with an infinity-style reflecting pool greets you at the visitor center, along with patchwork-style grassy areas and a manicured footpath.

Public tours and open houses are available with a reservation from spring until early summer, but the Temple is open for seasonal events throughout the year, including the Festival of Lights from December through January. The Temple has hosted the event since 1978 and it features live music, guest speakers, and an outdoor nativity scene.

Best time to visit: Christmas

Pass/Permit/Fees: Free

Closest city or town: Bethesda

Address: 9900 Stoneybrook Dr., Kensington, MD 20895

GPS Coordinates: 39.0141° N, 77.0656° W

Did You Know? The Washington Temple is the 18th LDS temple in the world.

Washington National Cathedral

When Pierre L'Enfant first designed Washington, D.C., he designated an area for a national church. It would take 100 years before plans for a national cathedral were ever put into motion and nearly another 20 more before construction would start. Today, the Washington National Cathedral fulfills L'Enfant's vision.

Officially known as the Cathedral Church of Saint Peter and Saint Paul, the National Cathedral is the American version of Westminster Abbey. It is a prayer house and historical monument for all people, hosting both religious and secular events throughout the decades. Tour the grounds of the Cathedral and appreciate the Gothic architecture. The gargoyles are something to marvel at. Inside, you'll find sculptures of George Washington, Rosa Parks, Mother Teresa, and more, among the beautiful arched ceilings and stained-glass windows.

Best time to visit: Summer

Pass/Permit/Fees: $10 per adult, $6 for students, seniors, and children

Closest city or town: Bethesda

Address: 3101 Wisconsin Ave., NW, Washington, D.C. 20016

GPS Coordinates: 38.9306° N, 77.0708° W

Did You Know? The Canterbury Pulpit is where Martin Luther King Jr. delivered his last sermon before his assassination.

Betterton Beach

Betterton Beach is a great spot for family vacations. The shores, however, are only open to tourists for a portion of the year. From April to October, visitors are welcome to surf, fish, jet ski, boat, and otherwise soak up the sun along the five-acre waterfront.

The small fishing village of Betterton became a coastal destination during the height of steamboat transportation in the late 19th century. Piers, boardwalks, and hotels popped up along the coast to entice travelers between Baltimore and Philadelphia.

Visitors can enter the beach at the mouth of the Sassafras River, which is less salinized than other parts of the Chesapeake and much more delightful to swim in. If you're bringing a boat, head to the public landing at the pier.

Best time to visit: May and June

Pass/Permit/Fees: Free

Closest city or town: Betterton

Address: Betterton Beach (Ericsson Ave.), Betterton, MD 21610

GPS Coordinates: 39.3710° N, 76.0636° W

Did You Know? Betterton Beach is the one beach in Maryland where you won't get stung by a jellyfish. The water isn't salty enough.

Allen Pond Park

A day of outdoor adventure awaits at Allen Pond Park. Start slowly by feeding the ducks or casting a fishing line. Picnic spots circle the water, or you can hit the trail for snug spots and gazebos tucked into the tree line. Allen Pond Trail is an easy .7-mile hike around the water with a paved path and plenty of nature to explore along the way. Bikes and pets are welcome on the trail, too.

If you prefer more of a workout, take the fitness trail or rent a paddleboat. Kids of all ages are welcome to climb and play on the equipment in Opportunity Park, with playground facilities for pre-school and school-age children as well as a basketball court. The Bowie Skate Park and Bowie Ice Arena are also located in the 85-acre park with public skating, special events, and more.

Best time to visit: Spring and summer for perfect picnic weather

Pass/Permit/Fees: Park and in-line skate park are free; $10 boat rentals; $6 public ice skating; fishing license required

Closest city or town: Bowie

Address: 3330 Northview Dr., Bowie, MD 20716

GPS Coordinates: 38.9344° N, 76.7374° W

Did You Know? The pond originally belonged to James Allen, a tobacco farmer who sold annual visiting passes to the pond for $10.

Belair Mansion

Maryland is host to numerous historical homes, but Belair Mansion is one such property that became more than just a house. It had not-so-humble beginnings as a plantation and governor's mansion when its original owner, Samuel Ogle, was elected Governor of Maryland in 1732. It again served as the governor's mansion in 1798. In 1747, Ogle brought the first English-bred thoroughbred racing horses to Maryland: Queen Mab and Spark. Selima arrived later and would go on to win the 1752 Derby, taking home the biggest prize of that century: 2,500 *pistoles*, roughly $750,000 by today's standard.

However, by 1957, then-owner William Jaird Levitt sold the mansion and surrounding acreage to the city of Bowie for $1 under the condition that the mansion would be used as City Hall. Today, visitors can step back in time with a tour of the home and the property, which features original furniture and items owned by the mansion's many residents.

Best time to visit: Spring and summer

Pass/Permit/Fees: Free; donations accepted

Closest city or town: Bowie

Address: 12207 Tulip Grove Dr., Bowie, MD 20715

GPS Coordinates: 38.9660° N, 76.7467° W

Did You Know? Spark, one of the first racehorses in America, was a gift from Prince Frederick to Samuel Ogle.

Belair Stable Museum

A visit to the Belair Mansion also means a tour of the stable museum. The museum consists of the property's original stables, including the Belair Stud Stable built in 1907, and the stablemaster's living quarters. After the Civil War, when the mansion was sold to settle Ogle family debts, the property continued to breed racehorses until it fell into disarray.

By the turn of the 20th century, the Belair Mansion was back on top, with horses placing over 1,700 times in races from 1923 - 1953. But horse racing had begun on this property long before then. Original owner Samuel Ogle wanted to bring English racehorses to America to ultimately improve the racing stock in the States, and he was successful. His prize mare Selima still lives on in the bloodlines of numerous Kentucky Derby winners, and the museum is visited every year by race enthusiasts, animal lovers, and history buffs alike.

Best time to visit: Spring and summer

Pass/Permit/Fees: Free

Closest city or town: Bowie

Address: 2835 Belair Dr., Bowie, MD 20715

GPS Coordinates: 38.9665° N, 74.7434° W

Did You Know? Belair stud jockeys wore distinct white and red polka dot jerseys to stand apart from the other racers.

Belt Woods

This 610-acre National Natural Landmark is home to the last of the old-growth white oak trees and tulip poplars on the East Coast. The property of Belt Woods originally belonged to Seton Belt, a descendant of Maryland's original settlers. Per his will, Mr. Belt ordered that his farm never be sold, and the trees never cut down. Unfortunately, by 1981, a New Jersey logging firm had earned legal rights to cut down the forest for veneer. A group of conservationists rallied to protect the forest, and today visitors can see these trees the way they were meant to be seen.

The oaks soar nearly a hundred feet up before reaching out their massive branches, which are home to a large population of forest birds, including Wood Thrushes and Kentucky Warblers. Hiking and hunting are allowed, but trails are not marked, and some are in poor condition, so proceed with caution.

Best time to visit: Spring for the blooms and the birds; November - January for hunting

Pass/Permit/Fees: Free; hunting license required

Closest city or town: Bowie

Address: Church Rd., Bowie, MD 20721

GPS Coordinates: 38.9068° N, 76.7614° W

Did You Know? The oldest trees in Belt Woods are at least 200 years old.

Bowie Railroad Museum

The Bowie Railroad Museum is a tiny gem tucked away in a small Maryland town. The railroad station remained in operation until 1989, and the City of Bowie restored the old building and turned it into a museum in the early 1990s.

Children will love playing on the old caboose out front, and history buffs will appreciate the old town's heritage and artifacts displayed in the tiny museum.

This museum will barely take you an hour to explore, but you have plenty of time before it opens to grab breakfast or brunch nearby. Or, better yet, due to the number of delicious seafood restaurants in Bowie, it's recommended that you visit one of them for lunch after working up a historical appetite in the museum.

Best time to visit: As soon as it opens at noon

Pass/Permit/Fees: Free; donations accepted

Closest city or town: Bowie

Address: 8614 Chestnut Ave., Bowie, MD 20715

GPS Coordinates: 39.0071° N, 76.7792° W

Did You Know? The Bowie Railroad Station was replaced by the Bowie State University Station, which is still in operation today.

Bowie Town Center

For a modern experience, visit the Bowie Town Center and indulge in your favorite urban delights. Shopping, dining, sips, and sweets line the street, and weekly Zumba classes and car shows mean there's something available for everyone.

Summer concert series host free live music, and children are invited to monthly tea parties, craft classes, and even virtual events hosted online at the Bowie Town Center website. If shopping or crafting isn't your thing, consider testing your wits at an escape room or pamper yourself at the salon. Store sales, deals, and center events will vary throughout the year, so check online to get coupons and find out which events are happening the next time you're in town.

Best time to visit: Depends on your interests

Pass/Permit/Fees: Parking is free

Closest city or town: Bowie

Address: 15606 Emerald Way, Bowie, MD 20716

GPS Coordinates: 39.0068° N, 76.7791° W

Did You Know? The mall's original stores were Sears, Hecht's, Barnes & Noble, Old Navy, Bed Bath & Beyond, and Best Buy.

National Capital Radio & Television Museum

This tiny museum in Bowie features exhibits that are displayed in a turn-of-the-century storekeeper's home, was refurbished by the city long before the idea for a broadcasting museum came up. Serendipitously, it turned out to be the perfect spot for this charming museum. The National Capital Radio & Television Museum explores the history of broadcasting through seven well-organized exhibits, starting with the wireless age of Morse Code.

Other sections explore the development of sound effects and the interesting tools used to bring early radio shows to life. What began as a few hobbyists' tiny collections of antique radios, this museum is now a historical showcase that doubles as a radio repair shop and collectible store for other hobbyists. The self-guided tours are small and intimate, and you can sign up for radio repair classes.

Best time to visit: April and May

Pass/Permit/Fees: Free

Closest city or town: Bowie

Address: 2608 Mitchellville Rd., Bowie, MD 20716

GPS Coordinates: 38.9263° N, 76.7333° W

Did You Know? The museum hired its first paid professional staff in 2011.

Prince George's Stadium

If you can't make it to Baltimore to see the Orioles play, catch a minor league game at Prince George's Stadium. The Bowie Baysox are the Orioles' Double-A affiliate, so you may recognize some players soon when they go pro. The stadium is equipped for 10,000 spectators and hosts events for groups of 10 to 2,500 people. Prince George's also holds vintage game events, car shows, fireworks, and more for the general public throughout the baseball season.

But more than baseball is happening at Prince George's. It is host to the annual Allen Iverson charity softball game, lacrosse tournaments, cricket games, and even community yard sales. During the off-season and away games, the stadium doubles as a drive-in theater and is known for offering movie nights throughout the year.

Best time to visit: April - September

Pass/Permit/Fees: Game tickets are $10 per adult, $7 for children and seniors

Closest city or town: Bowie

Address: 4101 Crain Hwy., Bowie, MD 20716

GPS Coordinates: 38.9450° N, 76.7098° W

Did You Know? Since 2020, the stadium has become the alternate training site for the Orioles.

Six Flags America

Six Flags America in Maryland is an exciting amusement park. Try the Mind Eraser, an inverted coaster that flies 115 feet up on tangled steel just to drop you down a 90-foot curved loop. The Superman Ride of Steel will drop you from 205 feet. It inspired a new name for rides that have drops of 200 feet or more, and this inverted hyper-coaster zips you around loops and twists at 73 mph.

There are also rides and activities in the park that don't involve fast roller coasters. Visiting in the summer means Hurricane Harbor will be open, where you can swim and waterslide until the sun goes down.

Best time to visit: May - December

Pass/Permit/Fees: $80 per person; purchase tickets online for up to 60% off

Closest city or town: Bowie

Address: 13710 Central Ave., Bowie, MD 20721

GPS Coordinates: 38.9061° N, 76.7726° W

Did You Know? The fastest and highest roller coaster in the country is Kingda Ka at Six Flags New Jersey.

Wincopin Green, Red, & Yellow Trail

The Wincopin Trail is broken up into three sections marked with green, red, or yellow blazes. The trail starts on the red path and hikers can choose which way they want to meander. Trails are marked with wooden signposts, making it easy to distinguish which path you are taking.

In total, the trail covers a 3.5-mile loop, passing both the Little and Middle Patuxent Rivers. At one point on the trail, the rivers will be on either side of you. The trail is also completely shaded, making it a popular summer hike among locals and tourists.

If you're hiking the trail, bring binoculars. Rare dragonflies and butterflies can be spotted near the water in the spring, along with multiple species of wildflowers and fungi. Notable birds to watch for include pine warblers, Kentucky warblers, and hooded warblers.

Best time to visit: Spring

Pass/Permit/Fees: Free

Closest city or town: Bowie

Address: 9299 Vollmerhausen Rd., Jessup, MD 20794

GPS Coordinates: 38.9438° N, 76.6981° W

Did You Know? Every April, Project Clean Stream comes to clean up Little Patuxent River.

National Museum of African American History and Culture

The National Museum of African American History and Culture is within walking distance of the Washington Monument and sits directly across the street from the Smithsonian Museum of American History. It is the newest and one of the best museums in D.C. It's usually very crowded. Tours are free, but timed tickets are required. Get yours early to get in without waiting in line.

Your tour will begin with an elevator ride to the lowest level. These exhibits focus on the Atlantic slave trade and how it shaped America as a nation. As you climb, exhibits showcase the Tuskegee Airmen, segregation and the Civil Rights Movement, and President Obama's campaign office.

Best time to visit: September - December

Pass/Permit/Fees: Free

Closest city or town: Capitol Heights

Address: 1400 Constitution Ave., NW, Washington, D.C. 20560

GPS Coordinates: 38.8911° N, 77.0326° W

Did You Know? It took nearly a century to build this museum, starting with the first bill to Congress in 1915.

International Spy Museum

Do you think you have what it takes to join the CIA? Check out the International Spy Museum and see. You can't miss it; it's the red-and-black building on L'Enfant Plaza in downtown D.C. As soon as you enter, you'll be debriefed and given a cover identity with which you can freely roam the museum. The museum displays over 1,000 artifacts of espionage, from ancient Egypt to present day, giving visitors a thorough debriefing on the history of espionage, the gadgets used by early spies, and how these covert operations have evolved over the centuries.

You'll get a peek into modern cyber espionage and discover how these secrets become intelligence. Whether it's George Washington's spies from the Revolutionary War or clever gadgets that rival anything in James Bond's arsenal, all four floors of the museum feature unique exhibits.

Best time to visit: Before 11 a.m. or after 4 p.m. to avoid crowds

Pass/Permit/Fees: $25 for adults, $23 for seniors and military, $17 for children

Closest city or town: Capitol Heights

Address: 700 L'Enfant Plaza, SW, Washington, D.C. 20024

GPS Coordinates: 38.8839° N, 77.0255° W

Did You Know? The museum was built by a former codebreaker and spy, Milton Maltz.

Jefferson Memorial and Tidal Basin

The Jefferson Memorial is a few blocks from the National Mall. It sits on the Potomac River, away from the rush of downtown D.C., and offers up a tranquil view of the tidal basin. Visitors are welcome to climb the stairs into the memorial or simply lounge against them and enjoy the view. The Jefferson Memorial was the vision of President Roosevelt. However, when construction began in 1938, no design for the memorial had ever been approved. Many locals protested, even chaining themselves to the cherry trees nearby to stop its construction until a design that protected the surrounding area was agreed upon.

If you want to brave the crowds during cherry blossom season, the Jefferson Memorial is the premier spot. Due to its placement on the river, visitors can follow the path along the water directly under the blooms. Arrive early to catch a meditative moment at the reflection pool before the tour groups arrive.

Best time to visit: March - April

Pass/Permit/Fees: Free; $2.30/hour for street parking

Closest city or town: Capitol Heights

Address: 16 E. Basin Dr., SW, Washington, D.C. 20242

GPS Coordinates: 38.8814° N, 77.0365° W

Did You Know? The monument's design is based on Jefferson's own design of UVA.

National Air and Space Museum

IAt the Smithsonian Institute's Air and Space Museum, rotating exhibits focus on the history and science of flight — including spaceflight — as well as the role aviation plays in exploration, research, art, and military affairs.

Past exhibits have included artifacts from Neil Armstrong and Buzz Aldrin's trip to the moon, a full recreation of scenes from 2001: A Space Odyssey, and Leonardo DaVinci's original artistic conceptualizations of human flight. Visitors can also see famous military jets and spacecraft not displayed anywhere else. If the sky isn't quite your limit, go beyond and explore the universe with the museum's unique collection of exclusive artifacts, including pieces of the Lunar Module LM-2 and planetary images from NASA rovers.

Best time to visit: September - December

Pass/Permit/Fees: Free

Closest city or town: Capitol Heights

Address: 600 Independence Ave., SW, Washington, D.C. 20560

GPS Coordinates: 38.8882° N, 77.0199° W

Did You Know? The *Enola Gay* drew more visitors than any exhibit during its short three-year display.

National Mall and Veterans Memorials

The National Mall spans two miles, from the Lincoln Memorial to the west side of the U.S. Capitol, and it includes everything in between. The most popular sites at the National Mall are the Washington Monument, Lincoln and Jefferson Memorials, Martin Luther King Jr. Memorial, and the Capitol building. It is entirely possible to see all of the monuments in one day but come prepared during the summer as there is little shade and a lot of crowding.

Best time to visit: Mornings, from September - November

Pass/Permit/Fees: Free; cost to park can vary; $5 for D.C. Metro

Closest city or town: Capitol Heights

Address: National Mall, Washington, D.C.

GPS Coordinates: 38.8875° N, 77.0364° W

Did You Know? An aerial view of the National Mall makes it appear to be designed in the shape of a Templar knight's shield.

National Museum of Natural History

Natural history includes rocks, plants, animals, and dinosaur bones, which there are plenty of at the National Museum of Natural History. Animal bones make up the second-floor exhibit, and visitors are invited to compare and contrast the different skeletons. Natural history also includes the impact of humans, and current exhibits on the first floor of the museum showcase the role Africa has played for the globe, from the art and culture that define its people, to the unique animals and ecosystems that make up the continent. Continue upstairs for more on Ancient Egypt. We are all interconnected through our natural history, and unique interactive exhibits throughout the museum encourage visitors to consider the role they play as they explore different animal kingdoms, walls of insects, and different socio-cultural artifacts.

Best time to visit: Early mornings in fall; the museum opens at 10 a.m.

Pass/Permit/Fees: Free

Closest city or town: Capitol Heights

Address: 10th St. and Constitution Ave., NW, Washington, D.C. 20560

GPS Coordinates: 38.8913° N, 77.0261° W

Did You Know? The museum is home to the famous Hope Diamond.

Smithsonian American Art Museum and National Portrait Gallery

The feeling at these two galleries is unlike anything you'll experience at an art museum anywhere else. The goal of the American Art Museum and National Portrait Gallery is to tell the story of America by showcasing the portraits of and artworks by the people who shape the nation. The American President's Gallery is a must-see at the National Portrait Museum. On your way up to the second floor, you'll pass *The Four Justices*, a portrait of the first four women on the Supreme Court. And don't miss the portrait of Katharine Hepburn in the 20th Century Americans exhibit.

Both the Portrait Gallery and the American Art Museum are housed in the former U.S. Patent Office, so you can easily see both in one day. Art featured in the American Art Museum include Mickalene Thomas's paintings and Do Ho Suh's sculptures.

Best time to visit: In the morning or early afternoon

Pass/Permit/Fees: Free

Closest city or town: Capitol Heights

Address: 8th and G Streets, Washington, D.C. 20001

GPS Coordinates: 38.8978° N, 77.0230° W

Did You Know? J.P. Morgan and H. C. Frick were among the first portraits in the gallery.

The John F. Kennedy Center for the Performing Arts

The Kennedy Center is host to symphonies, plays, ballets, concerts, and more throughout the year. But you don't need a ticket to explore the rooftop terrace, the REACH, the Grand Foyer, or the Hall of States. The Grand Foyer is in the main building with the Opera House, Concert Hall, and Eisenhower Theater. See the art in the Foyer and try to find your home state flag in the Hall of States. Nearby, the REACH is a unique "living theater" that incorporates the audience with performances, art, collaborations, and classes.

Victura Park at the REACH is an outdoor beer garden open from Thursday - Sunday. Beer, wine, and cocktails are available, and there are picnicking and grilling spots throughout the garden and along the river. Explore the menu at Victura, as it always changes with each new guest chef.

Best time to visit: Late spring

Pass/Permit/Fees: Free; $65-$99+ for events and concerts

Closest city or town: Capitol Heights

Address: 2700 F St., NW, Washington, D.C. 20566

GPS Coordinates: 38.8958° N, 77.0557° W

Did You Know? Eleanor Roosevelt was the first to propose a national performing arts center.

The Lincoln Memorial

Sit on the steps of the Lincoln Memorial and soak in the view of the Washington Monument in the reflecting pool. No matter the time of year or time of day, you will find people relaxing on these steps. Visiting in the morning means fewer crowds and a quiet walk around the pool. Designed by Henry Bacon and built in 1922, the Lincoln Memorial honors the 16th President of the United States. Some view him as the savior of the nation, and the symbolism can be found throughout the memorial. The 36 columns represent the 36 states in the union at the time, and the inscriptions on the north and southside of the interior are of the Gettysburg Address and Lincoln's second Inaugural Address.

Along with the inscriptions is a mural painted by Jules Guerin representing key moments of Lincoln's life that led him to become the country's steadfast leader during the tumultuous Civil War.

Best time to visit: Fall

Pass/Permit/Fees: Free

Closest city or town: Capitol Heights

Address: 2 Lincoln Memorial Cir., NW, Washington, D.C. 20002

GPS Coordinates: 38.8893° N, 7.0502° W

Did You Know? The sculpture of Lincoln took four years to complete.

The United States Capitol and Capitol Hill

The U.S. Capitol Building was once the geographic center of Washington D.C., which is why all of the district's numbered streets originate from here. It operates as the working seat of the U.S. Congress as well as a museum, art gallery, crypt, and restaurant. Visitors are welcome to tour the building for free.

The tour begins at the visitor center which houses temporary exhibits explaining the inner workings of Congress, featuring photographs of and handwritten letters by former presidents, senators, and representatives. The tour continues into the crypt, National Statuary Hall, and the Rotunda. If you want to see Congress in session, you will have to send a request to your congressman. The free, public tours of the Capitol Building do not include the Senate and House galleries.

Best time to visit: March - May

Pass/Permit/Fees: Free; passes required for special events

Closest city or town: Capitol Heights

Address: First St., SE, Washington, D.C. 20004

GPS Coordinates: 38.8860° N, 79.9995° W

Did You Know? Thomas Jefferson held a design contest for the Capitol and the White House. The winner received $500 and property in Washington, D.C.

The Washington Monument

At one point, the Washington Monument was the tallest building in the country, standing at 555 feet high. It almost wasn't built when there weren't enough funds available during the Civil War. You can see where construction halted during the war due to the different shades in the marble about 150 feet up. The monument is designed to represent an Egyptian obelisk and inspire the same sense of awe and respect early Americans felt for their first president. A trip to the very top gives visitors a 360-degree view of the National Mall, including sights of the White House and Capitol Building.

Due to its height, the top viewing deck is often closed during thunderstorms and high winds. To reach the top, visitors must reserve a ticket online in advance. Tickets are not available for same-day visits, and no tickets are given out at the memorial.

Best time to visit: September - January

Pass/Permit/Fees: Free; $1 to reserve a ticket to the top

Closest city or town: Capitol Heights

Address: 2 15th St., NW, Washington, D.C. 20024

GPS Coordinates: 38.8895° N, 77.0353° W

Did You Know? The original design included a circular building, but due to lack of funds, only the obelisk was constructed.

Lake Tuckahoe State Park

Completely slip away from the urban hustle and bustle and spend a few days at Tuckahoe State Park. Swimming is not allowed at Lake Tuckahoe, but fishing and boating are permitted. Anglers can catch a rainbow medley of fish, including yellow perch, black and white crappie, and pumpkinseed sunfish. If you fish near the stumps and roots by the shore, you might pick up a pickerel.

Animals are welcome at Tuckahoe State Park, including horses and dogs. Dogs must remain leashed at all times but are allowed on the hiking trails, campsites, and around the water. Take a horse on the equestrian hiking trails around the park. There is also a self-guided nature trail for families and a physical fitness trail. Camping is not available at the lake, but the public campgrounds are just a few yards away past the Cherry Lane Pavilion. Day camp programs are also offered for children in the summer.

Best time to visit: May - November

Pass/Permit/Fees: Free; $20-$70/night to camp

Closest city or town: Centreville

Address: 13070 Crouse Mill Rd., Queen Anne, MD 21657

GPS Coordinates: 39.2756° N, 74.7304° W

Did You Know? Tuckahoe Lake was originally built to power an old grist mill.

Calvert Cliffs State Park

Calvert Cliffs State Park is named after the massive natural formations that jut out into Chesapeake Bay. When dinosaurs walked the earth, these cliffs were under water. Today, they tell the story of all the creatures who lived before, and beachcombers can find prehistoric shark teeth and fossils of fish, whales, stingrays, and seabirds. No one is allowed to climb or hunt for fossils on the cliffs, but you are welcome to comb the sand or any boulders that have fallen from the cliffs. The best spots for fossils are at the northern end of the beach, which you can get to on the trail leading from the parking lot. There are 13 miles of hiking trails in total at Calvert Cliffs, with the Red and Orange trails being more difficult.

Best time to visit: At low tide, either from March - May or September - November

Pass/Permit/Fees: $7 per vehicle, $5 for Maryland residents

Closest city or town: Chesapeake Beach

Address: 10540 H.G. Trueman Rd., Lusby, MD 20657

GPS Coordinates: 38.3956° N, 76.4293° W

Did You Know? Calvert Cliffs were originally known as Rickard's Cliffes, which John Smith named after his mother.

National Gallery of Art

The National Gallery and Sculpture Garden at the National Mall is home to the only painting Leonardo daVinci ever created in the Americas. It also houses famous sculptor Alexander Calder's largest mobile, which hangs from the ceiling in his gallery. The original collection was donated by Andrew W. Mellon, famous American businessman and philanthropist. Other famous original donors include Paul Mellon and Chester Dale.

Today the collection has grown to include some of the most famous works by renowned artists. Tour through Renaissance and neoclassical paintings by El Greco, Rembrandt, and Frans Hals, and don't miss the rare print collections which include rare, illustrated books. Once you're finished inside, you can tour the sculpture garden on the grounds showcasing modern pieces by Claes Oldenburg, Coosje van Bruggen, Louise Bourgeois, and more.

Best time to visit: Arrive when the museum opens at 11 a.m. to get an early ticket

Pass/Permit/Fees: Free

Closest city or town: College Park

Address: Constitution Ave., NW, Washington, D.C. 20565

GPS Coordinates: 38.8913° N, 77.0200° W

Did You Know? This is the only free art museum in D.C.

Annapolis Rock

As it's one of the most popular hiking spots in Maryland, you will want to hit the Annapolis Rock trail as early as you can manage. Start at the trailhead in Myersville and hike for about two miles before veering left on the path to Annapolis Rock.

The trail is not clearly marked. Only a small sign will point you in the right direction, and you might miss it. Luckily, there isn't a bad view on this trail, so even if you take a few extra steps, it'll be worth it. Explore even further and hike the additional mile to Black Rock for two amazing views in one. Annapolis Rock is one stop on the Appalachian Trail, and you may pass a few AT-hikers on your way up to the Rock. Keep your eyes out for rock climbers and campers, and you may even spot an eagle.

Best time to visit: Weekday mornings in late spring and early summer

Pass/Permit/Fees: Free to hike and camp; camping is on a first-come-first-serve basis

Closest city or town: Columbia

Address: 11175 Baltimore National Pike, Myersville, MD 21773

GPS Coordinates: 39.2812° N, 77.1316° W

Did You Know? You can hike the 40-mile stretch of the Appalachian Trail through Maryland in five days.

Lake Elkhorn

Although it's not for swimming, Lake Elkhorn is a popular spot in Maryland among locals for the pleasant hiking trail along the water. The 3.4-mile loop features wildflowers in the spring, and the paved path makes it the perfect hike for families, pets, and bikers. Fishing is allowed on the water, along with boating, and the lake is stocked with trout each spring in preparation for the busy summer season. Nearby picnic pavilions and a playground make it the ideal place to stop for an afternoon, cast a line, and relax in the shade.

Lake Elkhorn barely reaches fifteen feet at its deepest point, but it's still not surprising to find snakes and turtles mucking about near the waterline. The lake is also home to unique species of dragonflies, including Twelve-Spotted Skimmers and Amberwings.

Best time to visit: April - June

Pass/Permit/Fees: Free

Closest city or town: Columbia

Address: 7200 Dockside Ln., Columbia, MD 21045

GPS Coordinates: 39.1831° N, 76.8422° W

Did You Know? Four drowning deaths in the lake led to a heated debate about its proximity to the nearby neighborhood.

National Cryptologic Museum

Cryptology — or the study of codes and how to write or decrypt them — is integral to espionage and cybersecurity concerns across the globe. In the United States, the National Security Agency (NSA) is responsible for encrypting and decrypting messages, documents, and more across cyberspace. The National Cryptologic Museum showcases some of the NSA's work as well as how cryptology has evolved in the age of the personal computer.

Historical exhibits focus on the Cold War and the development of supercomputers and satellite technology. Learn what kinds of languages are used most often in encryption and how biometrics work in data protection. Unlike the International Spy Museum which displays all manner of sneak artifacts, the artifacts on display at the National Cryptologic Museum relate specifically to the mathematics, linguistics, and technology used in historic and modern encryption to facilitate espionage.

Best time to visit: Weekday mornings; museum opens at 9 a.m.

Pass/Permit/Fees: Free; donations accepted

Closest city or town: Columbia

Address: 8290 Colony Seven Rd., Annapolis Junction, MD 20701

GPS Coordinates: 39.1148° N, 76.7747° W

Did You Know? Museum docents are retired NSA employees.

Symphony Woods

Merriweather Park and Symphony Woods host free summer concert series and annual summer events. Symphony Woods encircles the Merriweather Post Pavilion, which is a premier concert venue in Maryland, offering a variety of bands, orchestras, ballets, and other performances.

While Symphony Woods and the Chrysalis Lawn are packed during summer events, it's relatively quiet during the rest of the year. Visiting during the off-season or in-between special events in the summer gives you the park to yourself, providing ample opportunity for picnic lunches and naps in the shade. If you plan on seeing any concerts in Maryland, explore the listings at Merriweather and Symphony Woods to get the full experience.

Best time to visit: Summer

Pass/Permit/Fees: $20 per vehicle; event prices can vary

Closest city or town: Columbia

Address: 10431 Little Patuxent Pkwy., Columbia, MD 21044

GPS Coordinates: 39.2099° N, 76.8623° W

Did You Know? It's called Symphony Woods because it was originally intended to be the summer home of the National Symphony Orchestra.

Rocky Gap State Park

Rocky Gap State Park is home to Lake Habeeb, the 243-acre lake that boasts the bluest water in the state. During the summer, the lake fills up quickly, as does the rest of the park, and it's recommended you arrive early to secure a spot along the water. Camping is available, and there are over 3,000 acres and 278 campsites to explore. Choose from primitive spots, electric hookups, yurts, and cabins, as well as a family site that can accommodate groups of up to 40 people. Around the campgrounds, visitors can enjoy playgrounds, rent kayaks and canoes, and visit the Scales & Tales Aviary, an environmental program that features raptors, owls, turtles, and reptiles. No matter what you plan to do, Rocky Gap State Park offers something for everyone. Explore nature on the hiking trails, climb to the top of Evitts Mountain via the Evitts Homesite Trail (8 mi), or try your luck at the Rocky Gap Resort & Casino.

Best time to visit: Summer

Pass/Permit/Fees: $6 per person, $4 for Maryland residents

Closest city or town: Cumberland

Address: 12900 Lake Shore Dr., Flintstone, MD 21530

GPS Coordinates: 39.7056° N, 78.6535° W

Did You Know? Evitts Mountain is named for an early pioneer to Maryland who built his homestead atop the mountain.

Harriet Tubman Museum & Education Center

Harriet Tubman was born into slavery in Dorchester County, and it is now the site of her museum and educational center. Exhibits focus on the Underground Railroad as well as what life was like before, during, and after the Civil War for both enslaved and free peoples.

Harriet Tubman is universally recognized for organizing and freeing slaves with her secret network, but this skill of hers proved invaluable during the Civil War where she worked as a spy and a nurse. The mural at the front of the museum, painted in 2019 by Michael Rosato, emphasizes her altruism and invites you in to learn more. The museum/education center is just one stop on the Harriet Tubman Underground Railroad Byway, a self-guided driving tour following her life, including Brodess Farm and Bucktown General Store.

Best time to visit: Weekends

Pass/Permit/Fees: Free; donations accepted

Closest city or town: Dorchester County

Address: 424 Race St., Cambridge, MD 21613

GPS Coordinates: 38.5693° N, 76.0791° W

Did You Know? Harriet Tubman is the first American woman to lead an armed expedition in a war.

McKeldin Switchback Trail

Hop on the McKeldin Switchback Trail from the contact station near the entrance of Patapsco Valley State Park. This muddy trail is rated moderate, but hikers of all ages and skill levels can handle the path along the water. The hardest part is the steep switchback, but there are stairs to help your journey.

Bikers may have to avoid the northernmost part of the trail due to the terrain, but they can head to Plantation Trail (1.4 mi) and continue the loop from there. In total, McKeldin Switchback covers 4 miles and is one of the longest trails in Patapsco Valley.

Come during the late spring to catch sight of the tiny waterfalls descending from the rock outcroppings in their full glory or bundle up for a winter hike and catch the best view over the Liberty Dam Overlook at the end of the trail.

Best time to visit: April - September

Pass/Permit/Fees: $5 per vehicle

Closest city or town: Ellicott City

Address: 11676 Marriottsville Rd., Marriottsville, MD 21104

GPS Coordinates: 39.3599° N, 76.8931° W

Did You Know? McKeldin Trail is named after former Baltimore Mayor Theodore R. McKeldin.

Breezy Point Beach

When you don't feel like facing the traffic on the Chesapeake Bay Bridge, take a trip to Breezy Point Beach instead. The surf may not be as epic as at some other beaches, but Breezy Point is quiet, less crowded, and provides a separate camper's beach space for anyone staying overnight.

Breezy Point campgrounds are available on a first-come-first-serve basis and will quickly fill up during the summer and on holiday weekends. The beach will close once it reaches capacity, and those who leave will not be allowed back in. Boating and jet skis are not allowed at the beach, but the shore is open for swimming and fishing. Anglers can fish in the designated fishing area or cast a line off the 200-foot pier. Crabbing is also allowed from the pier.

Best time to visit: Early in the morning; the beach opens at 9 a.m.

Pass/Permit/Fees: $20 for non-residents, $10 for residents; $12/$6 per child of non-residents and residents, respectively

Closest city or town: Essex

Address: 5300 Breezy Point Rd., Chesapeake Beach, MD 20732

GPS Coordinates: 39.2776° N, 76.3844° W

Did You Know? Jellyfish are popular at this beach, and they will not hesitate to sting you.

Cherry Beach Park

Grab your kayak and hit the water at Cherry Beach. No swimming is allowed, but visitors can paddle their way up and down the Nanticoke River. You can enter the river from the boat ramp or the soft landing, but the water is deep and the current can get strong, so paddling with the current is advised. For those not interested in water activities, stay dry on the playground equipment and pack a lunch to enjoy beneath the picnic pavilion. Fishing is allowed in the Nanticoke with proper licensing, and you can fish from the shore or from your canoe.

Cherry Beach is across from Cope Bennett Park, which you can reach from a stone walking path beneath the bridge. No canoes or kayaks are allowed, but Cope Bennett boasts more playgrounds, picnic tables, two tennis courts, and a walking trail along the river.

Best time to visit: Late summer to early fall

Pass/Permit/Fees: Free; fishing license required

Closest city or town: Federalsburg

Address: 110 Cherry Beach Rd., Sharptown, MD 21861

GPS Coordinates: 38.5455° N, 75.7196° W

Did You Know? The Nanticoke River was mapped out by John Smith during his first exploration.

Carroll Creek Park

You would have no idea that the beautiful brick pathways making up Carroll Creek Park are actually protecting the city of Frederick. The city sits in the middle of a natural floodplain and, in 1976, a catastrophic flood left downtown under 3 feet of water. Thanks to Carroll Creek Park, the river now runs underneath the city, popping up every so often in the Galleria and East/West Fountains.
The trail along the water is a 1.8-mile loop open to hikers, bikers, walkers, families, and pets.

If you walk the whole loop, stop and appreciate the local art installations throughout, including sculptures at the suspension bridge and a bronze cast drinking fountain. Visitors can veer off the path at any point to visit the breweries, specialty shops, local restaurants, and even a local distillery along the way.

Best time to visit: Spring and early summer

Pass/Permit/Fees: Free

Closest city or town: Frederick

Address: Carroll Creek Linear Park, Frederick, MD 21701

GPS Coordinates: 39.4128° N, 77.4084° W

Did You Know? The city plans to add 550,000 square feet to the park in the future.

Catoctin Mountain Park

The Catoctin Mountain Range is Maryland's share of the Blue Ridge Mountains, and hikers can explore the wilderness on one or more of the park's eight trails.

Visit the east side of the park to hike to natural monuments like Chimney Rock and Hog Rock or travel the historical trails to the Blue Blazes Whiskey Still or through the Charcoal Exhibit Trail up to Thurmont Vista. The west side offers up the longest trails in the park: Orange Trail (10.5-mile loop) and Catoctin National Recreation Trail (9.5-mile loop).

Catoctin Mountain Park is also home to the president's famed vacation spot, Camp David. You won't be able to get close to the Presidential Retreat, but you can take advantage of the campgrounds, fishing spots, and picnic areas nearby.

Best time to visit: Fall

Pass/Permit/Fees: Free

Closest city or town: Frederick

Address: 14707 Park Central Rd., Thurmont, MD 21788

GPS Coordinates: 39.6341° N, 77.4502° W

Did You Know? The park was established in 1935 as part of an initiative to get Americans back to work after the Great Depression.

Chesapeake and Ohio Canal

Between 1828 and 1850, the Chesapeake and Ohio Canal (or "The Grand Old Ditch" as it's affectionately called) operated 74 locks on the Potomac River. Boats carrying all of the necessary supplies for a burgeoning nation traveled easily between D.C. and Maryland. The towpath of the canal is now a recreational and historical park where visitors can fish, swim, camp, and hike through this integral part of Maryland's early history.

The 184-mile path follows the canal through to Cumberland. Hikers and bikers can choose to stay near the water or veer off into other parts of Maryland on the Capital Crescent Trail or hop onto the Appalachian Trail at mile marker 58. Get off the beaten path and travel the canal by water on any of the four paddling trails. The Thompson Boat Center can set up beginners with paddling classes, Fletcher's Boathouse offers guided tours, and expert kayakers can hit the Kayak Run or take in the sights of Great Falls.

Best time to visit: Summer

Pass/Permit/Fees: $10 per vehicle, $5 per person

Closest city or town: Frederick

Address: 40 W. Potomac St., St. Brunswick, MD 21716

GPS Coordinates: 39.6006° N, 77.8264° W

Did You Know? C&O Canal is supposedly haunted, with ghost sightings in Paw Paw tunnel, the Monocacy aqueduct, and Big Pool.

Chesapeake & Ohio Canal National Historical Park

President Eisenhower established the Chesapeake & Ohio Canal as a National Monument in 1961 to protect and preserve the canal's original structure and surrounding buildings. The park encompasses 20,000 acres of history along the Potomac River, including the towpath that was once used by mules to tug and guide ships through the canal in the 19th century. Earlier attempts to revitalize the canal were thwarted by blizzards, political disagreements, and World War II, but today the canal is protected by national law and the local C&O Canal Association.

Camping is free at C&O National Historical Park. These spots are first-come-first-serve, and they can fill up quickly in the summer. Fortunately, you don't need to stay overnight to take advantage of the hiking trails and rock-climbing opportunities throughout the park.

Best time to visit: April - September for historical boat rides on the canal

Pass/Permit/Fees: $10 per vehicle, $5 per person

Closest city or town: Frederick

Address: 11710 Macarthur Blvd., Potomac, MD 20854

GPS Coordinates: 39.6006° N, 77.8264° W

Did You Know? The canal was originally supposed to reach Pittsburgh through an 8.4-mile tunnel through the Allegheny Mountains.

Cunningham Falls State Park

There are two ways to reach Cunningham Falls from the state park entrance: Lower Trail offers up beautiful views and easy terrain on a well-maintained gravel path, and Cliff Trail has rougher terrain with the opportunity to rock climb.

Hikers can't lose either way. Each trail leads to the 78-foot waterfall, and if you look closely, you'll see an old homestead at the top of the falls, a historic leftover from the early settlers for which the falls were originally named. (You may hear locals still refer to it as McAfee Falls.)

The loop to the falls and back is 1.1 miles, which gives you plenty of time to enjoy Big Hunting Creek which is a premier trout fishing spot, and Hunter Creek Lake nearby.

Best time to visit: Late spring or early fall

Pass/Permit/Fees: $5 per person, $3 for Maryland residents

Closest city or town: Frederick

Address: 14039 Catoctin Hollow Rd., Thurmont, MD 21788

GPS Coordinates: 39.5973° N, 77.4495° W

Did You Know? Hiking Bob's Hill Trail in spring is your best chance to see Maryland wildflowers in bloom.

Gambrill State Park

Sneak away from the city and see Maryland in a brand-new way. Gambrill State Park is tucked away in Frederick, kept like a secret up on Catoctin Mountain while offering up breathtaking views of the forests and valleys below. RVs are welcome to the electric hookups, and there are tent-only sites and cabins for everyone else to get comfortable.

Campers can reach the sites via the Red Maple Trail (1 mi) or take the longer hike through Cunningham Falls to Catoctin Mountain Park via Catoctin Trail (3 mi). Stay a few days to explore all 16 miles of trails throughout the park or make a day of it with a picnic and a tackle box. No matter how long you decide to stay, don't miss the view from the overlook at High Knob, which you can reach by driving a few miles past the parking lot. You can also access the trails throughout High Knob, which is good news when the parking lot is full during peak season.

Best time to visit: April - October

Pass/Permit/Fees: $5 per vehicle, $3 for Maryland residents

Closest city or town: Frederick

Address: 8602 Gambrill Park Rd., Frederick, MD 21702

GPS Coordinates: 39.4646° N, 77.4976° W

Did You Know? Horseback riding is allowed on every trail in Gambrill except White Oak Trail.

Historic Downtown Frederick

There are 40 blocks to explore in historic downtown Frederick. You can start from the top at Third Street and work your way down to South Street, or you can start on the east side at East Street and work your way over to Bentz Street. Along the way, you will find a hodgepodge of 18th, 19th, and 20th-century architecture. Colonial cobblestone streets lead up to tattoo parlors and art galleries while history unfolds at your feet. Visit the Civil War Medicine Museum on Church Street or treat yourself to a spa day at one of the salons on Market Street.

If you can get downtown on the weekend, hop on the vintage Frederick trolley for a unique tour of the city. It only runs on the first Saturday of the month, so plan accordingly. If you miss it, you can catch a ride in one of the historic open-air horse-drawn carriages.

Best time to visit: Winter, for trolley rides, carriages, and holiday festivities

Pass/Permit/Fees: Free; garage parking is $1/hour, $12/day

Closest city or town: Frederick

Address: 19 E. Church St., Frederick, MD 21701

GPS Coordinates: 39.4154° N, 77.4099° W

Did You Know? Frederick was originally called Frederick Town when it was established in 1745.

Schifferstadt Architectural Museum

Schifferstadt, built in 1758, is the oldest home in Frederick. It represents the colonial architecture popular among German settlers at the time and features one of the original three cast iron stoves used to heat the home during the winter. Other iconic architecture in the home includes the tight, winding staircase to the second level and a wishbone-style chimney.

The home originally belonged to the Brunner family, German immigrants who arrived in 1736. They named the property after their hometown, and the eldest son built the brick home visitors can tour today.

Visitors are also welcome to explore the Heritage Garden, an homage to colonial kitchen gardens of the era. The garden was recognized in 2015 for its historical preservation and accuracy.

Best time to visit: Weekends

Pass/Permit/Fees: Free; donations accepted

Closest city or town: Frederick

Address: 1110 Rosemont Ave., Frederick, MD 21701

GPS Coordinates: 39.4236° N, 77.4292° W

Did You Know? The hand-crafted brick walls of the home are two feet thick.

Sugarloaf Mountain

When you visit Sugarloaf Mountain, you'll agree that it looks like a sweet mound of sugar. But it won't feel so sweet on the hike up to the summit. The steepest point is right at the beginning of the Orange Trail, but you can avoid it by taking the Green Trail to the Red Trail from the West View parking lot. Sugarloaf is a unique piece of geology in the Piedmont area. It is a monadnock, or hill, that is isolated from the rest of the neighboring mountain range. In this case, it is undetermined whether Sugarloaf is a piece of the Catoctin Mountains or the remnants of an ancient Appalachian mountain mass.

No matter where it comes from, the view from the top is worth the steep climb, and the hike back down will be much easier. Your descent down the Red Trail will lead you to the Blue and White Trails, which will take you to more beautiful views at the McCormack Overlook.

Best time to visit: April and May

Pass/Permit/Fees: Free; donations of $5 or more accepted

Closest city or town: Frederick

Address: 7901 Comus Rd., Dickerson, MD 20842

GPS Coordinates: 39.2692° N, 77.3952° W

Did You Know? The first map of the mountain was sketched in 1707.

Weverton Cliffs

Many call the hike to Weverton Cliffs one of the dreamiest overlooks in the state. The two-mile out-and-back trail starts with a steep incline as you climb up stone steps, and it continues uphill most of the way until you reach the overlook. Once up there, you won't want to leave. Soak in the view of the rolling hills and the rushing river before easing your way back down the cliff face.

To reach the overlook, don't take the first trailhead you see from the parking lot. Turn right onto the road instead and walk to the very end. You'll see the stone steps that start the trailhead. The path is very rocky and can get slippery when it rains. Hikers are advised to wear hiking boots with good traction or spikes. If you want a longer hike, hop onto the trail from the Harpers Ferry Train Station parking lot. It's across the pedestrian footbridge and will lead you nine miles along the C&O Towpath to the top of Weverton Cliffs.

Best time to visit: Late afternoon, in time to catch the view of the sunset

Pass/Permit/Fees: Free

Closest city or town: Frederick

Address: Appalachian National Scenic Trail, Knoxville, MD 21758

GPS Coordinates: 39.3323° N, 77.6765° W

Did You Know? Weverton Cliffs are the halfway point on the Appalachian Trail.

Wolf Rock & Chimney Rock Trail

Take the east entrance of Catoctin Mountain Park to hike the Wolf Rock and Chimney Rock trails. The trail to Chimney Rock is the most strenuous in the park, with narrow pathways and steep inclines, but the view from the top of the mountain peaks before you even see the rocks makes it worth it. Once you reach the summit, the trail will ease up a bit as it leads you to Chimney and Wolf Rocks before veering off into a steep decline back to the visitor center.

If it's raining or the path is wet, hikers are advised to wear boots with spikes or otherwise good traction. Give yourself ample time to enjoy the views on this trail and to have some fun climbing into the crevices at Wolf Rock and Chimney Rock. Overall, the trail is only 3.5 miles and shouldn't take more than a few hours.

Best time to visit: Late spring or early fall

Pass/Permit/Fees: $5 per person, $3 for Maryland residents

Closest city or town: Frederick

Address: Catoctin Visitor Center is located at14707 Park Central Rd., Thurmont, MD 21788

GPS Coordinates: Chimney Rock: 39.6295° N, 77.4330° W; Wolf Rock: 39.6340° N, 77.4378° W

Did You Know? Both Chimney Rock and Wolf Rock reach an elevation of over 1,400 ft.

Dans Mountain State Park

Multiple species of birds live in the Dans Mountain State Park forest, including rare songbirds and wild turkeys. Birdwatchers can catch sight of ovenbirds and scarlet tanagers in the spring, and hunters are allowed to catch a prize turkey in the fall.

Wildlife sightings can also include black bears, bobcats, and rattlesnakes, so hike and explore with caution. Hikers can take an easy stroll through the forest on the Dye School Trail (.7 mi), or simply drive to the top of Dans Rock Overlook for an amazing view of the forest.

Slip away from nature for a moment and take a dip in the Olympic-sized heated pool on top of the mountain. Picnic pavilions nearby are available for rent, and the Hill Run Group Campground is open from May through September.

Best time to visit: Spring and summer

Pass/Permit/Fees: $4 pool pass

Closest city or town: Frostburg

Address: 17410 Recreation Area Rd., SW, Lonaconing, MD 21539

GPS Coordinates: 39.5818° N, 78.8972° W

Did You Know? Foragers, be on the lookout: many species of wild edible mushrooms are nearby.

Jennings Randolph Lake

Spend summers in Maryland at Jennings Randolph Lake. The lake sits on the border between Maryland and West Virginia and provides an untouched patch of wilderness perfect for animal lovers, bird watchers, boaters, anglers, and campers. There are over 80 campsites at the lake, and 70 of them come with electric hookups. Every Saturday night, rangers put on a production at the amphitheater on the campgrounds, with both a playground and horseshoe pits nearby. Campers can stay for a few nights or a few weeks to enjoy swimming, boating, and water sports in the summer.

Hiking trails are open year-round, giving visitors a chance to birdwatch every season, with songbirds in the spring and migratory birds in the winter. Hit the Sunset Trail for panoramic views of the dam or learn about all the trees at Jennings on the ¾-mile High Timber Trail.

Best time to visit: April - October

Pass/Permit/Fees: Free; $22-$26/night to camp

Closest city or town: Frostburg

Address: 1700 Jennings Randolph Rd., Kitzmiller, MD 21538

GPS Coordinates: 39.4169° N, 79.1365° W

Did You Know? The lake was built by the U.S. Army Corps of Engineers.

Lake Habeeb

Avoid the crowds this summer and visit Lake Habeeb, one of the D.C. Metro area's best-kept summer secrets. The lake is quiet and rarely as crowded as the beaches or other more popular lakeside campsites in the state. It's also known for having the bluest water in the state. Lake Habeeb is the heart of Rocky Gap State Park. .

Visitors can swim, fish, boat, and hike the surrounding trails, starting with the Lakeside Loop Trail around the water. This long but easy 5.3-mile trail leads visitors through the different shoreline and forest ecosystems and features four footbridges. For an easier hike, take Canyon Overlook Trail (¾ mi) to the top of the gorge for an amazing view of the lake from above. Stay at the lake in any of the 278 different campsites nearby, including cabins, yurts, and even a chalet that can accommodate up to 8 people, featuring gas fireplaces and an outdoor campfire area.

Best time to visit: Summer

Pass/Permit/Fees: $3/$6 for winter/summer day passes; $2/$5 for Maryland residents

Closest city or town: Frostburg

Address: 12500 Pleasant Valley Rd., NE, Flintstone, MD 21530

GPS Coordinates: 39.7025° N, 78.6555° W

Did You Know? Military families can rent free camping equipment at Rocky Gap.

Blueberry Hill Local Park

Take the family and get outside at Blueberry Hill for fun. Picnic areas with grills and playgrounds are scattered across the park's 20+ acres, and picnic facilities are available to rent for events and parties.

Stretch your legs with a game on the full-size soccer field or shoot hoops with the family on the basketball court. If anyone fancies a night game of tennis or softball, there are lighted courts and fields throughout Blueberry Hill. The park closes at sundown except for the lighted areas, which are open until 11 p.m.

Best time to visit: Late morning or early afternoon

Pass/Permit/Fees: Free

Closest city or town: Gaithersburg

Address: 16617 Bethayres Rd., Derwood, MD 20855

GPS Coordinates: 39.1289° N, 77.1565° W

Did You Know? The original park was only 10 acres; the additional land was acquired in 1983.

Clopper Lake

Clopper Lake in Seneca Creek State Park is your summer fishing destination. The lake can reach depths of 18 feet in some areas, and you'll have your fill of largemouth bass after fishing here. Anglers may also snag a few catfish and tiger muskies as well. Fishing and picnic spots are available along the Clopper Lake Trail (3.3 mi), which loops around the water and offers up amazing views of the lake and surrounding forest. Bikes are allowed on the trail, but it will be very crowded during the summer.

Swimming is not allowed at the lake, and visitors are warned to wade at their own risk. Luckily, you don't need to get in the water to enjoy the scenery or the wildlife at Clopper Lake. Turtles, deer, and blue herons are always nearby.

Best time to visit: April - September

Pass/Permit/Fees: $5 per person, $3 for Maryland residents

Closest city or town: Gaithersburg

Address: 11950 Clopper Rd., Gaithersburg, MD 20878

GPS Coordinates: 39.1427° N, 77.2527° W

Did You Know? Clopper Lake was created by the damming of Long Draught Creek in 1975.

Crystal Grottoes Caverns

A quarrying crew discovered Crystal Grottoes Caverns by accident when their drill bits fell through the holes and into the cave. The crew blew the face off the cliff instead, and the caverns opened to the public in 1922.

The tour through the caverns is fairly moderate, but there is plenty of room to move around and explore. The Blanket Room, the largest in the cave, reaches twenty feet high and spans twenty feet wide, with beautiful limestone formations from the floor to the ceiling.

Crystal Grottoes has more limestone formations of stalactites, stalagmites, and flowstone per square foot than any other cave in the country, and it has been maintained since its discovery over a century ago. The tour only takes 30 minutes.

Best time to visit: May - September

Pass/Permit/Fees: $20 per adult, $10 per child; cash only

Closest city or town: Frederick

Address: 19821 Shepherdstown Pike, Boonsboro, MD 21713

GPS Coordinates: 39. 4982° N, 77.6768° W

Did You Know? The caverns remain at 54°F all year round.

Dawson Farm Park

Dawson Farm is half park and playground and half exploratory history. The park itself sprawls over seven acres, complete with playground equipment, picnic pavilions, and a nature trail. The property is dotted with historical farmhouses, the most noted of which is Dawson Farm.

Also known as Rocky Glen, the Dawson Farm farmhouse is actually two homes from two different centuries. The first two-and-a-half-story home was built in 1875, while the second with the hipped roof was built in 1912. Both homes boast architectural ornaments key to their time, and the 20th-century home features unique built-in furniture.

The Urban Wildlife Sanctuary at Dawson Farm Park is another must-see. It showcases the forest and the creatures who call it home, offering a free and educational look at the park's surrounding ecosystem.

Best time to visit: Late spring to early summer

Pass/Permit/Fees: Free

Closest city or town: Gaithersburg

Address: 312 Ritchie Pkwy., Rockville, MD 20852

GPS Coordinates: 39.0739° N, 77.1428° W

Did You Know? Dawson Farm was not added to the state historical register until 1985.

Lake Bernard Frank

Explore the seven miles of hiking trails around Lake Bernard Frank to reconnect with nature. The Lake Bernard Loop is 3.5 miles along the water with amazing views of the lake and wildlife.

Lakeside Trail leads to a quiet little creek, and Muncaster Trail ends in a field filled with wildflowers in springtime. Rock Creek Trail is a winding path that connects the lake with Lake Needwood nearby. But the best trail is probably Old Nasty Trail. It's a short and steep hike, but it leads to the Meadowside Nature Center.

Lake Bernard Frank is home to many species of wildlife, and you can get up close and personal with a few feathered friends at the nature center. It's completely free and offers visitors interactive nature experiences and a chance to meet eagles, hawks, and owls on the Raptor Deck.

Best time to visit: Spring and summer

Pass/Permit/Fees: Free

Closest city or town: Gaithersburg

Address: 15211 Avery Rd., Rockville, MD 20855

GPS Coordinates: 39.1064° N, 77.1144° W

Did You Know? Lake Bernard Frank is named after one of the co-founders of the Wildlife Society.

Rock Creek Regional Park

If you plan on visiting either Lake Needwood or Lake Bernard Frank, you'll be in Rock Creek Regional Park. Rock Creek is home to these two beautiful lakes and features 13 miles of trails, a treetop adventure park, golf course, archery range, and the Meadowside Nature Center.

Hike the trails at Rock Creek in order to see the numerous wooden pedestrian footbridges built across the park. Many of the trails loop around one (or both) of the lakes and many paths are paved, making them ideal for hikers and bikers.

While the longest trail, Rock Creek Hiker/Biker Trail, is the most popular, there are many shorter and easier trails for light hikes early in the morning. For a beautiful nature walk and bird watching, take the Rocky Ridge and Backbone Loop (.9 mi) around the water.

Best time to visit: Early spring and early winter

Pass/Permit/Fees: Free

Closest city or town: Gaithersburg

Address: 6700 Needwood Rd., Derwod, MD 20855

GPS Coordinates: 39.1221° N, 77.1345° W

Did You Know? There are more than 203 species of bird in Rock Creek Regional Park, including 23 species of waterfowl.

Rockville Town Square

This 12.5-acre urban oasis in downtown Rockville (near Gaithersburg) is a one-stop shop for culture, dining, and local events. All season long, Rockville Town Square hosts family-friendly events, from splash pad parties and outdoor concerts to ice skating and dance classes.

While you can shop to your heart's content, there is more than just retail in Rockville. Get inspired at the VisArts Center Gallery and then head off to paint your own pottery at Color Me Mine or get creative with woodworking at Hammer & Stain. You can even craft your own yogurt sundaes at Berry Cup.

If you're hungry and don't want to spoil dinner with dessert, stop into any of the 25 restaurants in Town Square. Whatever you're craving, whether it's sushi, hot wings, or dumplings, you'll be sure to find something to satisfy.

Best time to visit: Winter

Pass/Permit/Fees: Free; parking is free for two hours, then $1/hour

Closest city or town: Gaithersburg

Address: 30 Maryland Ave., Rockville, MD 20850

GPS Coordinates: 39.0860° N, 77.1510° W

Did You Know? The ice rink at Rockville is the largest outdoor ice-skating rink in Maryland.

Seneca Creek State Park

Seneca Creek State Park is your opportunity to get close to the Potomac River. The 6,300-acre park reaches out 14 miles to the riverbank, providing scenic hiking trails and picnic spots along the way. The Schaeffer Trail System links the park together with bike-friendly hiking trails that go on for 60 miles.

Other trails in the park will lead to Clopper Lake, a popular draw for anglers and nature enthusiasts. Hikers can catch sight of wildlife on the Long Draught Trail (1 mi), which features beaver dams, and Mink Hollow Trail (1.5 mi). Longer trails are available to hikers, bikers, and equestrians, including the Seneca Greenway, a 16-mile hike along the C&O Canal. You'll also have a chance to explore a piece of history on the Seneca Greenway, which leads to the Seneca Quarry. The quarry was built in 1868 and provided stone for the Smithsonian Castle.

Best time to visit: April - September

Pass/Permit/Fees: $5 per person, $3 for Maryland residents

Closest city or town: Gaithersburg

Address: 11950 Clopper Rd., Gaithersburg, MD 20878

GPS Coordinates: 39.1431° N, 77.2531° W

Did You Know? Scenes from *The Blair Witch Project* were filmed in Seneca Creek State Park.

Little Seneca Lake

The hiking trail at Little Seneca Lake isn't actually something you can walk on. Black Hill Water Trail requires a canoe or kayak to explore, and you can rent one from the boat ramp at the lake. On the trail, you can explore 17 miles of shoreline and closely view the waterfowl and wildlife. Blue heron and ospreys are popular in the area, and if you keep your eyes peeled, you might spy a bald eagle. They are known for making their nests near the lake, and lucky visitors might see baby eaglets in the spring. Laminated water trail maps are available at the visitor center for self-guided tours, but the naturalists at Little Seneca Lake offer guided pontoon boat tours by request. Tours accommodate strollers, wheelchairs, and families or groups of up to 20 people. Reservations are required.

Best time to visit: May - September

Pass/Permit/Fees: $5 per boat; fishing license required; free for pedestrians and bikers

Closest city or town: Germantown

Address: 20930 Lake Ridge Dr., Boyds, MD 20841

GPS Coordinates: 39.1914° N, 77.3001° W

Did You Know? You can't swim in Lake Seneca, but you can wade in nearby Seneca Creek.

Blairs Valley Lake

Swimming, fishing, and boating are available at Blairs Valley Lake. The season in which you visit will determine your water activities. During the summer months, the lake spreads across 32 acres and can reach depths of 18 feet. This is ideal for swimming, but not fishing.

Oxygen cannot reach depths past eight feet during the summer, and the lake's populations of largemouth bass, rainbow trout, yellow perch, black crappie, and brown carp dwindle. But during the winter, anglers can catch fish up to four feet in length or bigger. However, the Maryland Fishing and Boating Services puts size limits on certain breeds of fish, including tiger muskie and bass. Bring a boat or fish from the shore. No gas motors are allowed on the water, but electric boats are fine.

Best time to visit: Summer for swimming, winter for fishing

Pass/Permit/Fees: Fishing license required

Closest city or town: Hagerstown

Address: Blairs Valley Lake, MD 21722

GPS Coordinates: 39.6951° N, 77.9414° W

Did You Know? The Blairs Valley Dam was built specifically to create this recreational lake for both locals and tourists in 1968.

Quirauk Mountain

Quirauk Mountain is the highest peak in South Mountain State Park. To reach it, take the Appalachian National Scenic Trail at Wolfsville Road to Pen Mar Park. Hikers first traverse an old railroad grade before slowly ascending the slope of the mountain.

You'll also pass the Raven Rock Shelter and Raven Rock Cliffs on your way to the top. The peak reaches 2,150 feet, offering breathtaking views of the valleys and landscape below. Visitors will also be soaking up a piece of history from up there, as the 1862 Battle of South Mountain was a famous skirmish of the Civil War. There are many more opportunities to get onto the Appalachian Trail from South Mountain State Park, with trailheads at High Rock, Raven Rock, and Monument Knob.

Best time to visit: April and May

Pass/Permit/Fees: $13/day to camp

Closest city or town: Hagerstown

Address: Quirauk Mountain, Highfield-Cascade, MD 21719

GPS Coordinates: 39.6965° N, 77.5128° W

Did You Know? On the Quirauk summit is the broadcasting tower for local WETH and WAYZ radio stations.

Falling Branch Trail

Hike the half-mile Falling Branch Trail to swim at the base of Kilgore Falls. The swimming hole is small and intimate, with enough space for no more than 75 people. The parking lot is limited to 28 cars and reservations are required. The trailhead starts from the parking lot and leads directly to the falls. The path is narrow and is not accessible for wheelchairs or strollers. Large coolers are also not allowed on the trail, and there are no picnic tables or campsites nearby. This is strictly a hike and swim destination, and your time at the falls may come with a time limit.

However, waiting your turn to hike Falling Branch is worth it. The private and pristine beauty makes for the perfect summer vacation spot, and visitation limits protect the vegetation and soil from erosion and keep the falls crystal clear.

Best time to visit: April - October

Pass/Permit/Fees: Free

Closest city or town: Harford County

Address: 1026 Falling Branch Rd., Pylesville, MD 21132

GPS Coordinates: 39.6928° N, 76.4270° W

Did You Know? The trail continues across the falls, offering a slightly better view of the water.

Rocks State Park

Rocks State Park offers three unique park areas to explore, including a stop at Kilgore Falls and secret fishing holes in Hidden Valley. To start, enter the main part of the park at Deer Creek Valley. Here is where you'll find picnic pavilions, hiking trails, Deer Creek Rapids, and the famous King and Queen's Chair rock formations.

To get to the royal rocks, take the King and Queen's Chair Loop (3.2 mi) from the main area. Start this hike first if you plan on hiking all day, as you'll climb uphill most of the way there. The way back will be downhill, landing you back at the park office and parking lot. From there you can head to Falling Branch or Hidden Valley. Falling Branch is where you'll find Kilgore Falls via the Falling Branch Trail (1.3 mi), and you can reach the fishing spot at the river by taking the Hidden Valley Trail (1 mi) on the Hidden Valley side of the park.

Best time to visit: September - February

Pass/Permit/Fees: $5/$4 per person/vehicle; $3/$2 for Maryland residents

Closest city or town: Jarrettsville

Address: 3318 Rocks Chrome Hill Rd., Jarrettsville, MD 21084

GPS Coordinates: 39.6312° N, 76.4157° W

Did You Know? The King and Queen's Chair formations were featured in the film *Tuck Everlasting*.

North Beach

North Beach is located on the western shore of the Chesapeake Bay, and it offers seven blocks of waterfront property, including a fishing pier and boardwalk.

Locals can access the beach for free, but visitors will have to pay upon arriving. Passes cover the full day, and beachgoers are welcome to park their cars near the pier for easy access to restaurants and shopping as well as the shore. Stick around for the weekend to catch the Friday Night Farmer's Market and Classic Car Cruise-In during the summer. North Beach offers up more than the beautiful shoreline. History buffs can check out the Bayside History Museum for exhibits on the historical significance of the Bay and information about the fossils, shark teeth, and Native American artifacts found all over the shore.

Best time to visit: Summer

Pass/Permit/Fees: $9 per adult, $6 for children and seniors

Closest city or town: Lothian

Address: 8916 Chesapeake Ave., North Beach, MD 20714

GPS Coordinates: 38.7073° N, 76.5311° W

Did You Know? The first fire station at North Beach didn't open until 1926.

Muddy Creek Falls

Muddy Creek is the highest, single-drop waterfall in Maryland, dropping from the Youghiogheny River off a 53-foot gorge. It steals the show in Swallow Falls State Park by being the bigger and more beautiful waterfall, but you have to come during the spring to see it in its full glory. Visitors can reach Muddy Creek Falls on their way to Swallow Falls via the Swallow Falls Canyon Trail. Step off the 1.1-mile loop onto a wheelchair-accessible boardwalk to see Muddy Creek before continuing the rest of the way around the trail. Mountain bikers can lengthen the trail by hopping on the path to Herrington Manor State Park.

For more hiking trails, take advantage of Muddy Creek's home in Garrett State Forest and hop onto the Rock Maze Trail. It's a short and easy, albeit somewhat tricky, path through the old trees to a maze of boulders. The secret nooks behind the rocks are worth exploring.

Best time to visit: March - May

Pass/Permit/Fees: $5 per person, $3 for Maryland residents

Closest city or town: McHenry

Address: Maple Glade Rd., Oakland, MD 21550

GPS Coordinates: 39.4971° N, 79.4212° W

Did You Know? Cunningham Falls is technically taller than Muddy Creek but doesn't fall from a single drop.

Swallow Falls State Park

If waterfall hikes are what you're after, then visit Swallow Falls State Park. Muddy Creek Falls, Maryland's tallest free-falling waterfall, and Swallow Falls are the two main attractions, but there are plenty of tiny falls throughout the park that can really get flowing after the spring melt. There are two hiking opportunities that lead you to the falls. Canyon Trail is for foot traffic only and will take you to Muddy Creek Falls over a 1.25-mile trek through the old-growth forest.

Some of the hemlock trees here are over 300 years old and are the last of their kind. If you want to bike, the 5.5-mile Mile Trail will take you through the park and into nearby Herrington Manor State Park by way of the Garrett State Forest. It's a beautiful, easy ride with plenty of bird watching and wildlife sightings along the way. If you didn't bring a bike with you, rentals are available at the Herrington Manor.

Best time to visit: March - October

Pass/Permit/Fees: $5 per person, $3 for Maryland residents

Closest city or town: McHenry

Address: 2470 Maple Glade Rd., Oakland, MD 21550

GPS Coordinates: 39.4971° N, 79.4212° W

Did You Know? Thomas Edison camped here for two weeks in 1921.

Tolliver Falls

Tolliver Falls is one of the smaller, often overlooked waterfalls in Swallow Falls State Park. At barely five feet high, it is definitely overshadowed by Muddy Creek and Swallow Falls, but it does offer up a much more scenic area than its big brothers.

To get to Tolliver Falls, continue south on Canyon Falls Trail past Lower and Upper Swallow Falls. The trail will veer sharply to the right and away from the river before you find yourself nestled under a tree canopy with tiny Tolliver Falls. The tree canopy works wonders for your camera, making Tolliver much easier to photograph than the larger falls, and its off-the-trail location means it's less crowded and more serene. It's an excellent spot to sit and relax before heading back to the parking lot.

Best time to visit: October and November

Pass/Permit/Fees: $5 per person, $3 for Maryland residents

Closest city or town: McHenry

Address: Tolliver Falls, MD 21550

GPS Coordinates: 39.4948° N, 79.4189° W

Did You Know? During the fall, the rocks on the waterfall appear to change color to match the leaves.

Herrington Manor State Park

If you're looking for a place to camp in Maryland all year round, visit Herrington Manor State Park. The 365-acre recreational park hosts events every season and provides 20 log cabin rentals.

Swim and kayak in the summer, or come in the colder months for cross-country skiing, snowshoe lessons, and the annual Apple Butter Boil. Equipment is available to rent all season long as well, including skis, snowshoes, kayaks and canoes, and sleds.

Hikers should come in the spring, which is the best time to be on the trails in Maryland. There are 12 miles of trails in Herrington Manor, one of which crosses into neighboring Swallow Falls State Park. Other trails lead deep into Garrett State Forest, while some circle the lake.

Best time to visit: Fall, for the Apple Butter Boil

Pass/Permit/Fees: $4 per vehicle, $2 for Maryland residents

Closest city or town: Oakland

Address: 222 Herrington Ln., Oakland, MD 21550

GPS Coordinates: 39.4538° N, 79.4482° W

Did You Know? Herrington Manor did have an estate home on the property, belonging to Abijah Herrington, but it was razed in 1964 to establish the state park.

Assateague Island

Once upon a time, Assateague Island had big dreams of being a resort town. However, after numerous hurricanes and tropical storms, the community gave up on any hope for permanence. The beach continually changes width and length from summer through winter. Today, visitors are still welcome to enjoy the ever-changing two miles of beach on Assateague's shores. Swimming, surfing, fishing, and kayaking are encouraged, and so are leisurely strolls in the sand, hunting for seashells and shark teeth. You might also spy a deer or wild pony, a favorite sight on the island. You'll most likely catch them snacking on saltmarsh grass, so head to the marshiest areas of the island to get a peek.

Best time to visit: April - October to see the horses; September is the best time for surfing

Pass/Permit/Fees: Free on foot or by bicycle; $25/week per vehicle; $40/year for pass

Closest city or town: Ocean City

Address: 11800 Marsh View Ln. Berlin, MD 21811

GPS Coordinates: 38.0993° N, 75.2071° W

Did You Know? The horses on Assateague aren't really wild but rather feral descendants of domesticated horses left behind by 17th-century farmers.

Ocean City Beach

Ocean City Beach is one of the top ten beaches in Maryland. It costs nothing to spend all day here, and even on the busiest days, it's still possible to find a great spot along the 10 miles of manicured shoreline. Take in the sun and the surf or try a kayak or canoe. The beach starts at the south end with the boardwalk and works its way up to Midtown at 28th Street. Between 28th and 90th streets are the restaurants and nightlife, including the Jolly Roger Amusement Park.

All summer long, the town of Ocean City hosts multiple events, from movie nights on the beach to fireworks shows and live music. Check the city's website to plan your visit along with the town's scheduled events or join the boardwalk at any time for spur-of-the-moment activities.

Best time to visit: Summer

Pass/Permit/Fees: Free; $8 to use the pier

Closest city or town: Ocean City

Address: 1409 Boardwalk, Ocean City, MD 21842

GPS Coordinates: 38.3927° N, 75.0614° W

Did You Know? The local population of Ocean City is less than 8,000, but over 330,000 people can be in town on any one summer weekend.

Ocean City Boardwalk

The boardwalk is the most iconic part of Ocean City. It stretches for three miles up the beach. Catch a ride on the roller coaster or slow down and savor the view from on top of the Ferris wheel. You'll quickly see why it's voted one of the best boardwalks by National Geographic and the Travel Channel. Trimper's Rides, the 19th-century amusement park built in 1893, adds a vintage air to the place while novelty shops, local eats, and the eclectic Ocean Gallery art museum enhance the experience.

At night the boardwalk comes to life with live music and events. Throughout the summer, the boardwalk is host to family activities. There is always something happening, so you never have to worry about being too late or too early for anything.

Best time to visit: Late August to early September

Pass/Permit/Fees: $8 to use the pier

Closest city or town: Ocean City

Address: 1409 Boardwalk, Ocean City, MD 21842

GPS Coordinates: 38.3377° N, 75.0815° W

Did You Know? On August 6, 2021, Ocean City recorded the first-ever shark bite in Maryland history.

Mount Vernon

Mount Vernon was the home of the first American president, George Washington, but it was owned by the Washington family beginning in 1674. Washington acquired the lands in 1761 and maintained the estate during his presidency until his death in 1799. The estate is now owned and maintained by the Mount Vernon Ladies Association, which protected the home by having it declared a historic landmark in 1858. The Association offers tours of the property every day of the year. The best room on the tour is Washington's study, a room very few of his own contemporaries saw.

Other highlights include a marble chimneypiece in the large dining room and the boxwood trees in the gardens that were planted by Washington in 1786. Visiting Mount Vernon has been an American tradition since 1794, started by George Washington himself. He never objected to curious locals asking to tour the property, and that tradition continues today.

Best time to visit: Summer

Pass/Permit/Fees: $28 per adult; $15 for children

Closest city or town: Oxon Hill

Address: 3500 Mt. Vernon Memorial Hwy., Alexandria, VA 22309

GPS Coordinates: 39.7293° N, 77.1074° W

Did You Know? The original house was built by George Washington's father in 1734.

Billy Goat Trail

Billy Goat Trail is broken up into three different sections, each of varying skill levels. Section A is the most popular and the most strenuous, requiring hikers to scramble over boulders and climb a cliff face. Section B is a little easier with fewer boulder climbs, and Section C is the easiest.

The three sections of the nearly 5-mile trail are not directly connected but are casually linked together by the towpath along the C&O Canal. You can do all three, but realize that the end of Section C will drop you off 2¾ miles away from Section A.

Hikers can access the Section A trailhead from the Great Falls Tavern Visitor Center, but you will have to pay to enter the park. Section B and C trailheads start near the Carderock Recreation Area and do not have entrance fees.

Best time to visit: Weekday mornings

Pass/Permit/Fees: Free except for Great Falls Tavern, which is $20/vehicle, $10/person

Closest city or town: Potomac

Address: 11710 Macarthur Blvd., Potomac, MD 20854

GPS Coordinates: 39.0009° N, 77.2484° W

Did You Know? The construction of the C&O Canal was one of the last orders of President James Monroe.

Glenstone

Glenstone Contemporary Art Museum exclusively features artists from the 20th and 21st centuries. Collections include works by Carl Andre, Pino Pascali, Jackson Pollock, and hundreds more. Past exhibits featured the interactive experiences of Rirkit Tiravanija and Martin Puryear's labor-intensive wooden sculptures. The minimalist design of the museum itself inspires visitors to seek art and creativity both inside and out, but the interior of the museum isn't the only place to appreciate contemporary art. The grounds surrounding the museum are dotted with sculpture, architecture, streams, and nature trails.

Visitors are encouraged to explore as much outside as they do inside. The goal of Glenstone is to blend art, design, architecture, and nature into one contemplative space, to not only fully appreciate art but to also inspire those who walk the gallery to perhaps create something of their own.

Best time to visit: Early, when the museum opens at 10 a.m.

Pass/Permit/Fees: Free

Closest city or town: Potomac

Address: 12100 Glen Rd., Potomac, MD 20854

GPS Coordinates: 39.0618° N, 77.2531° W

Did You Know? To be featured in Glenstone, artists must have been exhibited for at least 15 years.

Battle Creek Cypress Swamp

This is the only large stand of trees on Maryland's western coast. Unlike a forest, which is a combination of different types of trees and vegetation, the Battle Creek Cypress Swamp is a stand of bald cypress trees. Hiking and bird watching here provide a rare close look at these trees and the wildlife living among them. The swamp is a designated National Natural Landmark. The Calvert Nature Society on-site offers nature studies and interactive exhibits for visitors at their center, which features a few raptors and a rare albino snapping turtle.

You can alsotake a walk on the Wetland Boardwalk and keep an eye out for waterthrush, green frogs, and spring peepers. Battle Creek Cypress Swamp is a must-see during the spring when the songbirds are singing, and the wildflowers are in bloom.

Best time to visit: Late spring and early fall

Pass/Permit/Fees: Free

Closest city or town: Prince Frederick

Address: 2880 Grays Rd., Prince Frederick, MD 20678

GPS Coordinates: 38.4900° N, 76.5918° W

Did You Know? The swamp is home to skunk cabbages, which are stinky flowers with leaves that smell like a skunk.

Grace Episcopal Church

This tiny church in the historical town of Mt. Vernon is a testament to the Carpenter Gothic architectural style of the mid-19th century. The church was built between 1846-1847 with a steep, gabled roof and an iconic three-bay window on the front wall. The attached cemetery was built at the same time and holds graves from the 19th and 20th centuries. Carpenter Gothic style is uniquely limited to private homes and churches in early America, mostly due to the abundance of timber at the time, which made it easy to mass-produce wood moldings.

The tiny town of Mt. Vernon is about 10 minutes from the larger town of Princess Anne. Both are listed on the National Registrar of Historical Places. Grace Episcopal Church is only five minutes from Mt. Vernon Beach.

Best time to visit: Fall

Pass/Permit/Fees: Free

Closest city or town: Princess Anne

Address: 1607 Grace Church Rd., Silver Spring, MD 20910

GPS Coordinates: 38.2428° N, 75.7689° W

Did You Know? Scottish novelist Sir Walter Scott is known for sparking the architectural Gothic revival that swept Europe and North America in the 19th century.

7 Locks Brewing

The music hits and the beer flows at 7 Locks. Every Saturday night, local bands light up the stage and local food trucks crank up the heat. The taproom crafts seasonal beer flavors to match the mood, including a strawberry Saison in the summer. The brews at 7 Locks come on tap and in a can, with flavors alternating by season and availability. The brewery's mission is to bring craft beer to the masses, and the flavors concocted here offer something for everyone over the age of 21. But don't mistake the brewery as just a bar. Stop in for a drink and catch the band, but don't miss any of 7 Locks Brewing's weekday events. Check the events calendar for pet adoptions, trivia nights, farmers' markets, and more.

Best time to visit: Spring and summer, when the taproom boasts new fusions

Pass/Permit/Fees: Free tastings happen throughout the year; check the brewing events calendar for specific annual dates

Closest city or town: Rockville

Address: 12227 Wilkins Ave., Rockville, MD 20852

GPS Coordinates: 39.0560° N, 77.1102° W

Did You Know? The Devil Alley IPA and Sandy Pointe Blonde Ale both won awards in the 2019 statewide craft beer competition.

Beall-Dawson Museum

Take a tour through a piece of 19th-century history frozen in time. In 1815, Upton Beall, then clerk to the Montgomery County court, wanted a home that would reflect his wealth and status in the unassuming farm town of Rockville. Ironically, Upton would die twelve years later, leaving the home to his wife and three daughters. The theme of three sisters owning the Beall-Dawson home became a tradition, with the surviving Beall daughter leaving the property to three of her cousin's daughters after she died.

Today, the home and museum are the seat of the Montgomery County Historical Society. The architecture of the home is a testament to the Federal style that dominated the United States throughout the 18th and 19th centuries. The house contains almost all of its original architectural details, as well as artifacts and antiques from the home and others of that time period.

Best time to visit: Weekends, when the library and Stonestreet Museum are open as well

Pass/Permit/Fees: Free

Closest city or town: Rockville

Address: 103 W. Montgomery Ave., Rockville, MD 20850

GPS Coordinates: 39.0847° N, 77.1553° W

Did You Know? You can explore a 19th-century doctor's office and library nearby.

Lake Needwood

Near Lake Bernard Frank, Lake Needwood features trees unique to the Piedmont area and offers up more wildlife sighting opportunities than its neighbor. Shorebirds can be seen when the water level is low, especially Canadian geese in the fall; and the water is stocked with catfish, bluegill, and largemouth bass.

The hiking trails at Lake Needwood are beautiful, but unfortunately none of them fully encircle the lake. Each trail around the water is interrupted by either Needwood Road or Gude Drive, but there are plans to extend some of these trails in the future.

In the meantime, you can use the Needwood hiker-biker trail, a paved path that leads from D.C. The trail technically terminates at Needwood, but you can choose to hike the trailhead from the water. It's the perfect hike for anyone looking to slip in and out of the urban hustle and bustle.

Best time to visit: September and October

Pass/Permit/Fees: $4 per person

Closest city or town: Rockville

Address: 15700 Needwood Lake Circle, Rockville, MD 20855

GPS Coordinates: 39.1252° N, 77.1305° W

Did You Know? Lake Needwood is contaminated with microcystin, so keep pets away from the water.

Matthew Henson Trail

The greenway in Matthew Henson State Park is one of the most popular and heavily trafficked trails in Rockville. The 4.4-mile paved trail starts near Rock Creek Trail, leading through the city, the forest, and the parkland. The path itself is 8-feet wide, which means there's plenty of room to share with the bikers, horses, and wildlife you're likely to run into.

Although it's a popular trail, you can still get some peace and quiet if you hike early in the morning or later in the afternoon. The trailhead can be easily accessed from the parking lot on Dewey Road, and the only time hikers and bikers cross a main street is at the pedestrian crosswalk at Veirs Mill Road. The trail is marked as easy, but the many tight turns and hills could slip up new riders. It can also get pretty steep if you're heading northbound, so be prepared.

Best time to visit: April - May

Pass/Permit/Fees: Free

Closest city or town: Rockville

Address: Veirs Mill Rd. east to Georgia Ave., Aspen Hill, MD 20906

GPS Coordinates: 39.0757° N, 77.0712° W

Did You Know? You can lengthen this hike by continuing onto Rock Creek Trail.

Antietam National Battlefield

Antietam was the scene of the bloodiest battle in U.S. history. Over 22,000 soldiers were dead or wounded by the time the battle ended with Confederate General Robert E. Lee retreating across the Potomac. Today, visitors can hike the battlefield and follow the course of the day-long battle across nine different trails. The Bloody Lane Trail (1.6 mi) leads from the visitor center through Mumma and Roulette Farms while the Cornfield Trail (1.5 mi) starts and ends at the North Woods.

Snavely Ford Trail (1.8 mi) is the easiest trail on the battlefield and even offers up a shady spot near the end of the trail. Three Farms Trail (3.2 mi) is the quietest and most beautiful, but it's also the longest. Tidball Trail (.6 mi) is the shortest and offers the best view from atop the overlook.

Best time to visit: Spring

Pass/Permit/Fees: $10 per person; $20 per vehicle

Closest city or town: Sharpsburg

Address: 302 E. Main St., Sharpsburg, MD 21782

GPS Coordinates: 39.4687° N, 77.7388° W

Did You Know? On the first Saturday in December, 23,000 lanterns are lit and lined up on the battlefield to honor the fallen soldiers.

AFI Silver Theatre and Cultural Center

If you're planning on seeing a movie in Maryland, see it here. The AFI Silver Theatre is the perfect combination of art and film in one place. The theater shows current films and remasters of the classics, with events and private screenings available throughout the year. AFI hosts three annual film festivals: AFI DOCS (summer), AFI European Union Film Showcase (winter), and AFI Latin American Film Festival (fall). AFI also hosts film series throughout the year, showcasing fresh voices and perspectives from today's film industry. See a movie in the 400-seat stadium theater or reserve one of the smaller, historical theaters and host an intimate screening. The theater is equipped to play the latest high-definition blockbusters, 70mm wide-screen gems, silent films, and everything in between.

Best time to visit: Weekday mornings for matinee pricing

Pass/Permit/Fees: $13 for general admission; $11 for members, seniors, military, students; $8 for children; $10 matinees

Closest city or town: Silver Spring

Address: 8633 Colesville Rd., Silver Spring, MD 20910

GPS Coordinates: 38.9966° N, 77.0725° W

Did You Know? AFI Silver Theatre is located inside the original Silver Theatre and was designed by John Eberson in 1938.

Gateway to NOAA

The National Oceanic and Atmospheric Association's headquarters are located in Silver Spring, giving locals and visitors a special treat when it comes to forecasting the weather and understanding the climate changes happening on our planet. The Gateway to NOAA is your opportunity to learn what NOAA does, the kinds of tools they use, and how the association navigates the relationship between the sea, the sky, the weather, the climate, and our environment. It is particularly important to Maryland, given the unique ecosystem of the Chesapeake Bay area.

Gateway provides a closer look at how coastal and ocean resources are protected in the state and invites visitors to ask questions at the Science on a Sphere explorer kiosk. The exhibit is completely free and self-guided, but guided tours can be scheduled in advance.

Best time to visit: Spring

Pass/Permit/Fees: Free

Closest city or town: Silver Spring

Address: 1325 East-West Hwy., Silver Spring, MD 20910

GPS Coordinates: 38.9932° N, 77.0312° W

Did You Know? The National Oceanic and Atmospheric Association was founded by President Nixon.

National Capital Trolley Museum

You can easily miss the tiny trolley museum in Silver Spring, but it's definitely worth the stop. Take a ride through the woods on a vintage streetcar and discover what it was like before personal vehicles.

The National Capital Trolley Museum has at least one of each kind of vintage streetcar ever used in Washington, D.C., and the surrounding area, including wooden 19th-century Capital Transit cars and trolleys built during WWII. The exhibit also includes international streetcars from Canada, Germany, France, and England.

Rides on the different trolleys are offered regularly throughout the year with special opportunities for school field trips in the fall. Tickets to ride can be purchased at the museum, but it's strongly recommended that you buy them online ahead of time as seats fill up quickly.

Best time to visit: Saturdays

Pass/Permit/Fees: $10 for adults; $8 for seniors and children

Closest city or town: Silver Spring

Address: 1313 Bonifant Rd., Silver Spring, MD 20905

GPS Coordinates: 39.0979° N, 77.0313° W

Did You Know? Streetcars first appeared in Washington D.C. in 1862 and were drawn by two horses.

National Museum of Health and Medicine

The National Museum of Health and Medicine is one of the more offbeat museums in Maryland. It was established during the Civil War to collect and research military surgery items and medicine, and now includes 5,000 skeletons, 8,000 preserved organs, and over 25 million medical and surgical artifacts. Skeletons, organs, and body parts all showcase different types of medical trauma, from injury to disease, and how modern medicine has evolved to treat these cases. Scientific exhibits showcase the largest collection of human embryos through every stage of birth and include some interesting artifacts, like the hairball found in the stomach of a young girl. The squeamish will not enjoy this museum very much, but people looking for an unconventional, educational experience are in for a real treat.

Best time to visit: The museum opens at 10 a.m.

Pass/Permit/Fees: Free

Closest city or town: Silver Spring

Address: 2500 Linden Ln., Silver Spring, MD 20910

GPS Coordinates: 39.0089° N, 77.0539° W

Did You Know? The violence and gore of the American Civil War inspired Surgeon General William Hammond to establish the museum to study it.

Silver Spring Library

Silver Spring Library sits on the corner of Wayne Avenue in downtown Silver Spring. The original library was established in 1931, but the current building was completed in 2015 to meet the growing educational demands of the community, with new technology and meeting spaces. The library stands seven stories high and offers a coffee shop, post office, county offices, and art studio space along with its collection of 90,000 resources, including children's books, teen resources, fiction, non-fiction, and more.

The new technology in the library features a teen-only Mac computer lab, a business lab, 47 public all-in-one computers with webcams, and two 3D printers. At this library, visitors can check out up to 100 items for 3 weeks. Unfortunately, library cards are only available to Maryland and D.C. residents, but the library itself is available to the public and anyone can use the facility during its open hours.

Best time to visit: May and June

Pass/Permit/Fees: Free

Closest city or town: Silver Spring

Address: 900 Wayne Ave., Silver Spring, MD 20910

GPS Coordinates: 38.9949° N, 77.0246° W

Did You Know? The new library cost $64 million to build.

St. Andrew Ukrainian Orthodox Cathedral

This church on New Hampshire Avenue is built in the traditional Kozak Baroque style, adding a level of beauty and ambiance to the neighborhood. It was erected in 1986, the same year as the Chernobyl nuclear disaster, and is dedicated to the victims. A mosaic of the church's Patron Saint Andrew sits above the front entrance.

Most of the parish is Ukrainian or of Ukrainian descent, and services are conducted in both Ukrainian and English. Visitors are welcome to enter the church, attend liturgy and confession on Sundays, or visit with the clergy by appointment. The Cathedral's Grand Hall is quite beautiful to see, but it is often reserved for weddings and events. If you would like a tour of the Cathedral, you must call and request an appointment.

Best time to visit: September for the annual Washington Ukrainian Festival

Pass/Permit/Fees: Free

Closest city or town: Silver Spring

Address: 15100 New Hampshire Ave., Silver Spring, MD 20905

GPS Coordinates: 39.1041° N, 77.0037° W

Did You Know? St. Andrew is the patron saint of Scotland and Russia.

Wat Thai Washington, D.C.

Wat Thai Buddhist Temple hosts the annual Songkran Festival every spring, offering delicious eats, educational resources, and camaraderie to visitors of all creeds. Local vendors selling Thai chili plants and more are at the festival. Come early, because the grounds at Wat Thai fill up quickly with hungry tourists and patrons waiting for mango sticky rice, boat noodles, BBQ pork and chicken, and other Thai treats. You do not need to be a practicing Buddhist to dig into this delicious feast, and guests are welcome to bring blankets and picnic on the temple grounds.

Outside of the festival, Wat Thai is not a typical tourist location. Visitors can enter the temple to pay their respects and explore the grounds, but it's unlikely to be as exciting as it will be during Thai New Year.

Best time to visit: April

Pass/Permit/Fees: Free to visit; cost for food and parking can vary

Closest city or town: Silver Spring

Address: 13440 Layhill Rd., Silver Spring, MD 20906

GPS Coordinates: 39.0770° N, 77.0469° W

Did You Know? In 2018, the Thai government expanded Songkran into a week-long celebration.

Wheaton Regional Park

There are fourteen different sections in Wheaton Regional Park. Between the botanical gardens, adventure park, carousel, hiking trails, horseback riding, and ice-skating rink, you're bound to find something fun to do. For starters, you can ride on the C.P. Huntington engine train for a tour of the woods and the meadow. Then stop for a picnic in the Shorefield area by Pine Lake. From here you can hike the nature trails or head off to the adventure playground for swinging, climbing, and sliding.

If you want to see some animals, visit the Brookside Nature Center to meet reptiles, raptors, and mammals. At Wheaton Park Stables, you can practice horseback riding or join the trainers for an escorted nature trail ride.The Orebaugh area contains a fenced-in dog park.

Best time to visit: April and May to avoid the summer crowds

Pass/Permit/Fees: Free; $1.75 to ride the train and carousel

Closest city or town: Silver Spring

Address: 2000 Shorefield Rd., Silver Spring, MD 20902

GPS Coordinates: 39.0519° N, 77.0431° W

Did You Know? Brookside Gardens is home to live butterflies for the Wings of Fancy exhibit.

Chesapeake Bay Maritime Museum

To get an even closer look at the historical significance of the Chesapeake Bay, visit the Maritime Museum in St. Michaels. It captures every part the Bay plays in Maryland, from its geological structure and its strategic military placement to the flora and fauna that call the Bay home. Visitors can explore the Hooper Strait Lighthouse and learn more about the lives of the boatmen who worked and lived there in the 18th and 19th centuries, including taking a closer look at 100 different boat and ship models that cruised the Bay.

If you visit during the summer, you can ride on the museum's replica buy-boat for a tour on the water. Don't miss your chance to build a skiff or practice seafood harvesting during the museum's "Apprentice for a Day" events. If you're lucky enough to catch it, the museum staff races their log canoe during the summer as well.

Best time to visit: Early, when the museum opens at 10 a.m.

Pass/Permit/Fees: $16 per adult, $13 for seniors and students, $12 for military, $6 for children

Closest city or town: Talbot County

Address: 213 N. Talbot St., St. Michaels, MD 21663

GPS Coordinates: 38.7881° N, 76.2206° W

Did You Know? Hooper Strait Lighthouse was not originally here and was barged sixty miles north to be preserved as part of the museum.

Gunpowder Falls State Park

Gunpowder Falls is the largest state park in Maryland, encompassing 18,000 acres of wetlands, mountains, and forest. The park is divided into six different areas, four of which are mainly used for hiking, biking, horseback riding, and camping. However, Hammerman Area is a wonderful family beach spot with playgrounds, picnic pavilions, and public swimming areas.

Over 120 miles of nature and hiking trails make up the park, the most popular of which is Sweathouse Branch and Wildlands Loop, a 4.7-mile trail that treats hikers to a quiet swimming hole at the end. Hikers will also see two meandering waterfalls, one of which is Big Gunpowder Falls, as they work their way around the loop. Dundee Creek Marina at the basin of Gunpowder River is another section popular with boaters, kayakers, and tubers in the summer.

Best time to visit: Summer

Pass/Permit/Fees: $7 per person, $5 for Maryland residents

Closest city or town: Towson

Address: 7200 Graces Quarters Rd., Middle River, MD 21220

GPS Coordinates:
39.3609° N, 76.3463° W

Did You Know? Anglers can try their luck in the creek, and archers are welcome to practice at the range nearby.

Patuxent River Park

Preservation of nature and wildlife is tantamount at Patuxent River Park. For this reason, the hiking and equestrian trails are unmarked and untended, although you can follow the trails pretty easily based on the hikers who have come before.

The north end of the park is where you'll find these social trails, and it's a popular spot with mountain bikers as well. Access the trailheads from the parking lot at the end of Brown Church Rd and along Long Corner Rd. If you want a more-developed route, visit the south end of the river to hike the Flowing Free Trail. The nature center is also down on the south end, and it offers guided hikes for visitors as well as interactive exhibits and activities for kids and families. Hunting and fishing are permitted in the designated areas with proper licensing.

Best time to visit: April - December

Pass/Permit/Fees: Free; fishing license required

Closest city or town: Upper Marlboro

Address: 16000 Croom Airport Rd., Upper Marlboro, MD 20772

GPS Coordinates: 39.2380° N, 77.0561° W

Did You Know? Out of the 6,700 acres in Patuxent, 1,579 are undeveloped wildlands.

Wheatley Lake

Wheatley Lake in Gilbert Run Park is stocked full of bass, bluegill, catfish, and crappie. Anglers are required to release any bass they catch but are welcome to keep any other fish that happen to bite their line.

There is no swimming allowed in the lake, but visitors can rent pedal boats and canoes from the park. The boat ramp gives visitors access to the water on their own terms, which will give you better access to fishing the deepest part of the lake by the dam. If you don't have a boat, you can drop your line off one of the piers instead. Around the water is Wheatley Lake Trail, a two-mile loop featuring pedestrian bridges and wildlife sightings. Wheatley is an ideal spot for birdwatching and features seasonal waterfowl along the water's edge during the spring and winter months.

Best time to visit: April - October

Pass/Permit/Fees: $5 per vehicle

Closest city or town: Waldorf

Address: 13140 Charles St., Charlotte Hall, MD 20622

GPS Coordinates: 38.4911° N, 76.8555° W

Did You Know? The lake is stocked with rainbow trout in winter.

Proper Planning

With this guide, you are well on your way to properly planning a marvelous adventure. When you plan your travels, you should become familiar with the area, save any maps to your phone for access without internet, and bring plenty of water—especially during the summer months. Depending on the adventure you choose, you will also want to bring snacks and even a lunch. For younger children, you should do your research and find destinations that best suit your family's needs. Additionally, you should also plan when to get gas, local lodgings, and where to get food after you're finished. We've done our best to group these destinations based on nearby towns and cities to help make planning easier.

Dangerous Wildlife

There are several dangerous animals and insects you may encounter while hiking. With a good dose of caution and awareness, you can explore safely. Here is what you can do to keep yourself and your loved ones safe from dangerous flora and fauna while exploring:

- Keep to the established trails.
- Do not look under rocks, leaves, or sticks.
- Keep hands and feet out of small crawl spaces, bushes, covered areas, or crevices.
- Wear long sleeves and pants to keep arms and legs protected.
- Keep your distance should you encounter any dangerous wildlife or plants.

Do not rely on cell service for navigation or emergencies. Always have a map with you and let someone know where you are and for how long you intend to be gone, just in case.

First Aid Information

Always travel with a first aid kit with you in case of emergencies.

Here are items to be certain to include in your primary first aid kit:

- Nitrile gloves
- Blister care products
- Band-aids - multiple sizes and waterproof type
- Ace wrap and athletic tape
- Alcohol wipes and antibiotic ointment
- Irrigation syringe
- Tweezers, nail clippers, trauma shears, safety pins
- Small Ziplock bags containing contaminated trash

It is recommended to also keep a secondary first aid kit, especially when hiking, for more serious injuries or medical emergencies. Items in this should include:

- Blood clotting sponges
- Sterile gauze pads
- Trauma pads
- Second-skin/burn treatment

- Triangular bandages/sling
- Butterfly strips
- Tincture of benzoin
- Medications (ibuprofen, acetaminophen, antihistamine, aspirin, etc.)
- Thermometer
- CPR mask
- Wilderness medicine handbook
- Antivenin

There is so much more to explore, but this is a great start.

For information on all national parks, visit: www.nps.gov.

This site will give you information on up-to-date entrance fees and how to purchase a park pass for unlimited access to national and state parks. This site will also introduce you to all of the trails of each park.

Always check before you travel to destinations to make sure there are no closures. Some hikes close when there is heavy rain or snow in the area, and other parks close parts of their land for the migration of wildlife. Attractions may change their hours or temporarily shut down for various reasons. Check the websites for the most up-to-date information.

Made in the USA
Middletown, DE
07 March 2024

51009992R00080